"Do all the good you can; By all the means you can,

In all the ways you can; In all the places you can,

To all the people you can; As long as ever you can." - John Wesley

The deepest craving of human beings is to be needed, to feel important and to be appreciated. Give it to them and they will return it to you tenfold - Anonymous

"The secret of change is to focus all of your energy, not on fighting the old, but on building the new." – Socrates

Dr. Krishnamurthy Iyer

14th March 2024

9+7 WAYS OF GETTING VOLUNTARY ACTIVE SUPPORT FROM PEOPLE AROUND US

*INCLUDING BOSSES, PEERS AND SUBORDINATES

DR. KRISHNAMURTHY IYER

Author – Top Three Secrets for Becoming a High Performer

Get Noticed & Get Promoted

INDIA • SINGAPORE • MALAYSIA

ISBN 979-8-89322-672-0

"Parent's love - it never fails or falters, enduring come what may, a miracle no one can understand, but which shines like the rarest and brightest of stars; the fuel that enables a human being to attain the impossible, the best mystery of creation, a gift unparalleled" - Anonymous.

This book is respectfully dedicated to,

my parents

and

my elder brother (Late) Shri S. Prakash.

Acknowledgements

I wish to express my gratitude to my wife, who inspired me to write about the experiences I had in my corporate life for 43 years. She invariably stood by my side when writing this book late into the nights. Her presence was a reminder that I should continue writing page after page while staying motivated in the journey.

My heartfelt thanks to Dr. R. P. Mohanty for having gone through my manuscript and suggesting many small and big changes - which I implemented, and the gain was all mine - his observations substantially enriched the text.

I wish to thank Dr. S. Rajagopalan for taking the time to go through my book draft and making some invaluable comments, which have duly been incorporated.

My salutations to Shri S.H Mane and Dr. Prince Augustin, my superiors in Crompton Greeves Limited and Mahindra & Mahindra Limited, respectively, for over a decade plus, in both companies, for my exposure, experience and learnings at middle and senior levels.

I wish to acknowledge Shri Asger Mulla, my longtime friend, for the diagrams with caricatures that appear in this book. His support has been invaluable.

My profuse thanks to Ms. Nirrmala Mennon, who helped me in getting the manuscript together. My gratitude to her for helping me in doing relevant and appropriate research wherever it was deemed necessary.

I would be failing in my duty if I do not gratefully acknowledge the role of Shri Anand Rajagopalan, who painstakingly helped me to complete the narration and ensure the manuscript was crisply knit together.

Finally, no book is ever complete without a foreword, for which I am grateful to Dr. R.P. Mohanty, my PhD guide, and Mr. Ranjit Mehra, my first boss and mentor at Crompton Greeves Limited, both of whom accepted my request to add very encouraging and insightful forewords, drawing upon their immense corporate, academic, and business experience.

I am profusely thankful to Notion Press, my publishers, for their professional approach, appropriate support and guidance in the publishing process.

Dr. Krishnamurthy Iyer

Foreword 1

SIKSHA 'O' ANUSANDHAN
(A Deemed to be University declared u/s 3 of UGC Act, 1956)
Re-Accredited by NAAC with 'A' Grade

FOREWORD

Professor R P Mohanty
B.TECH; M.TECH; MBA; Ph.D.; D.SC; FIIIE; FNAE; FORSI; FITEI; SMIISE.
CHIEF CONSULTANT & FORMER VICE-CHANCELLOR
SIKSHA 'O' ANUSANDHAN UNIVERSITY, BHUBANESWAR
KHANDAGIRI SQUARE, ODISHA - 751 030

I have known Dr. K. Iyer for the last 35 years. He came in my contact when I was the Professor and Dean in the National Institute of Industrial Engineering (NITIE), Mumbai (now known as IIM Mumbai). He was very kind in professionally involving me to deliver a number of lectures to senior/ middle level managers both in Crompton Greaves Ltd. and Mahindra & Mahindra Ltd in the areas of Engineering Management and Organisation Behaviour. We both became intimate because of my success in those programmes; and he wanted to pursue his doctoral degree under my supervision. He worked in the subject theme entitled "Adaptation of Japanese management methods in Indian Organisations". We were fortunate to conduct a few experiments in the factories of Crompton Greaves, where we collected data and interpreted some useful findings. We could learn a lot from Mr. K. K. Nohria, who was then the Managing Director. We further learnt from several eminent scholars in attending International Conference in Production Research (ICPR) particularly in Jeruselum (Israel). It is worthy to mention that his thesis examiner late Professor Ezey M Dar-el (Israel Institute of Technology, HAIFA) highly appreciated the research particularly the work on action learning concepts, applications and interpretations.

I am of the opinion that this book is definitely a brilliant learning outcome of several facets and aspects of Organisation Behaviour by Dr. Iyer. Moreover, the chapters are demonstrations of several experiments, which we conducted in the factory settings. I convey my hearty congratulations to Iyer for brilliant demonstration of his innovative ideas and lifelong learning out of his education and experiences in excellent companies in India.

Although, we do not teach voluntary active support in the course curriculum of Organisation Behaviour, but the various topics dealt in this book are worthy enough to be inclusive in the curriculum as examples of practice and action learning. Furthermore, the writings are simple/ lucid and exposition of some ground realities of professional life. I wish this book must serve as a reference guide to all corporate citizens to derive immense utilities.

January 27, 2024

(Prof. R. P. Mohanty)

Khandagiri Square, Bhubaneswar - 751 030, Odisha , India
Phone : 0674 - 2350635, 2350791, Fax : 0674 - 2350642, 2351842
www.soa.ac.in

Foreword 2

It is a privilege to have the opportunity to write a foreword for Dr. Krishnamurthy Iyer's second book titled *'9 + 7 Ways to Get Voluntary Active Support from People Around Us - including bosses, peers & subordinates.'* This book deals primarily with an ever-increasing dilemma that several aspiring middle-management professionals face in the business world today. They are perpetually in the pursuit of ways and means to hone their capabilities and skills to climb the corporate ladder.

The author and I have been colleagues for a long time, and I can vividly recall his display of dedication, a truly clear understanding of the job to be done, self-motivation, and the use of effective interpersonal management skills. All these vital factors have been responsible for his result-orientation with execution excellence. This book adequately deals with his later forays into the management ladder making it a 'must-read' and a value-add for every professional.

An Engineer by qualification, Dr. Krishnamurthy Iyer has enhanced his academic credentials with the acquisition of a Diploma in Management Studies and a doctorate in HR. This is an extremely coherent and advantageous combination encompassing the sheer practical and logical skills of engineering with the man-management skills of HR. His active association with the academic and training side of HR has added to his already illustrious list of achievements.

I have had the pleasure of reading this book multiple times and have no hesitation in recommending it to one and all. My best wishes to Dr. Krishnamurthy Iyer for all his future endeavours.

Ranjit Mehra

Ex-Whole-time Director & CEO

Borosil Glassworks Ltd.

Prologue

This book is written with practical constructs and insights from working in two major corporations for well over four decades. At Crompton Greeves Limited, I had the opportunity to work in diverse departments, starting with Production, Methods Engineering, Vendor Development, Projects, etc., and then transitioning to Personnel Management & Industrial Relations. I held the position of General Manager-HR for four major manufacturing plants in the Automotive Sector of Mahindra & Mahindra Ltd. I also had a long stint in Organisational Development, Learning & Development, and Internal Communications. This gave me a vast repertoire of challenging interpersonal and team situations wherein I was able to garner support from superiors, colleagues, and associates. Every single experience was a learning one for me, and I have intended to put many such examples in this book for the benefit of professionals at large.

I have captured the crux behind actions taken at different points in time and put them in the form of (9 + 7 = 16) ways to get Voluntary Active Support (VAS). This book contains the gleanings, with stories and practical suggestions buttressed by appropriate caricatures as to how one can get voluntary active support in professional life, family settings, and social domains.

In this book, I have attempted to present the methodologies to leverage VAS in enhancing personal effectiveness in groups and organisational effectiveness. I hope my humble attempt serves the purpose it is intended for. I have used a conversational style of writing to create an impact and to enable learning in an easily comprehensible manner.

The application of the principles mentioned in the book is the key to success.

I wish my readers happy, meaningful, and value-added learning.

Dr. Krishnamurthy Iyer

Contents

Chapter 1

The Origin – The Compelling Drive to write this Book

Often, in corporate life, I have observed executives face challenges in terms of getting support from people over whom they don't have direct authority. In addition, there are also constraints in terms of subordinates being assigned to managers early in their careers. This is the stage where we learn the ropes of getting Voluntary Active Support (VAS) from people around us. The main objective of writing this book is to share my experience in this area. This will help upcoming executives, as well as middle and senior-level people. **(The term VAS will denote Voluntary Active Support wherever it appears in this book).**

Passive support is almost guaranteed in organisations. We all have experienced this when people say, "I will do it," and then don't do it or pretend as if they never committed or create excuses not to keep to their promises despite repeated follow-ups. Active support is all about wilful involvement in the task, out of their own free volition. I have used several illustrations in the form of caricatures throughout this book, which would lend meaning and function as anchors, irrespective of whether they are in the corporate world or social and domestic settings.

Despite a plethora of readings available on this subject like *Influence Without Authority* by Allan R. Cohen and David L. Bradford or *The Speed of Trust, The One Thing that Changes Everything* by Stephen M.R. Covey, or *The Indian Boss at Work: Thinking Global Acting Indian* by Steve Correa, I have not come across any book which attempts to capture the basic tenets of VAS in the life of working professionals, in the home front or relations with friends, relatives and neighbours. The 9 + 7=16 ways outlined in this book, simply and lucidly, provides readers with insightful experiences and recommend ways to implement the learnings.

I consider it important to leave a legacy in terms of the experience gained in my journey from a Production Engineer to a Behavioural Scientist. For simplicity and to enhance retention, the content is presented in a mix of images, diagrams, captions, and one-liners to make reading interesting for everyone who browses through it.

Chapter 2

Voluntary Active Support (VAS) – Explained

Zero and One Principle

Let us draw an analogy from computer language wherein we have a 0 and 1 as the bit and byte language. Let us consider '0' as the self and '1' as the other person. When we build a structure in computer language, we have 01, 0001, 11011 and so on. In the same manner, in an organisation, proper interaction between the '0' that is the self, and the several '1's we keep interacting with, sets the right chemistry, for achievement of desired outcomes.

The dictionary meaning of voluntary is 'chosen with intent,' and here, active can be defined as 'involved, committed and enthusiastic.' 'Passive Support' from organisation members, in any case, is guaranteed as people are on the payroll. People do not refuse, but at the same time the job is not getting done or completed.

However, to get VAS from people, some skills are essential, some of which have been outlined in this book. In simple words, when one gives active support from his or her own volition, would be termed as Voluntary Active Support.

For example - suppose I ask person A: "I want something urgently," and he says, "I will definitely let you know when I can do it," or "let me think over it," etc. Added to this, I may have to do repeated follow-ups. This would be **passive support**. On the other hand, if he seeks necessary clarifications and does the job on or before time, this would be **active support.**

Chapter 3

Linkage of Attitude with Behaviour & Performance

There is a very close relationship between attitudes, behaviour, and performance.

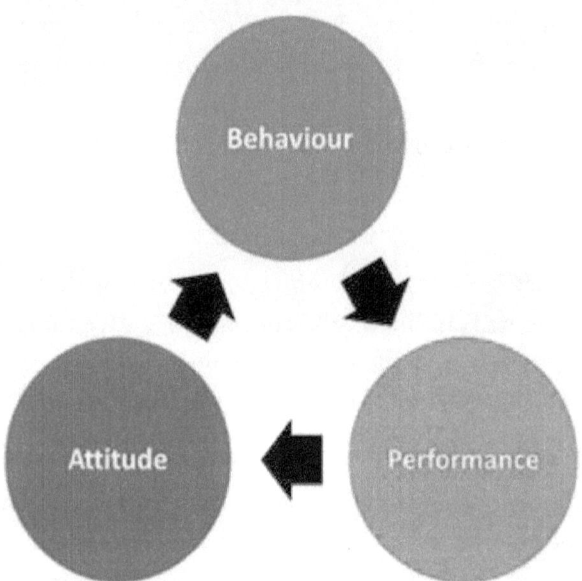

(Figure no. 1: Linkage of Performance with Behaviour)

Attitudes shape behaviour, and behaviour leads to performance. We shall first talk about attitudes. Attitudes are mainly formed from three sources.

- 1st - from actual experience/personal experiences

- 2nd - from hearsay

- 3rd - from social media and the environment one is exposed to.

My attitude is the way I look at people, events, or situations. There are two filters through which our attitudes are formed. They are 1) our value systems and 2) our belief systems. This is explained in detail with the help of the figure below:

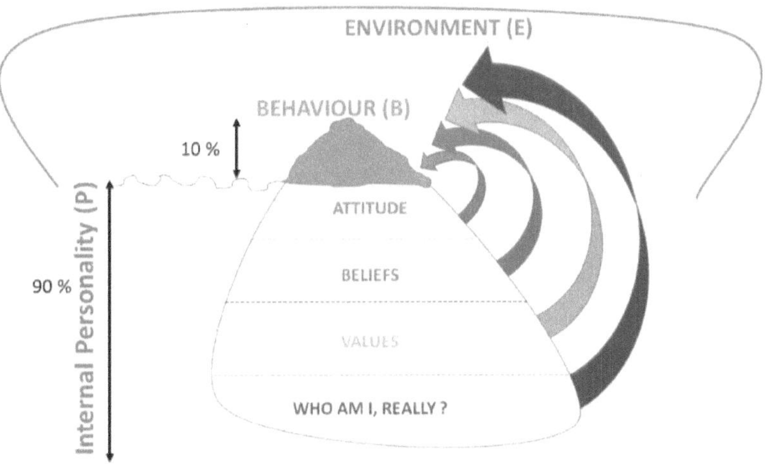

*(Figure no. 2: Iceberg showing relationships among personality, behaviour
& environment)*

In the iceberg above, 10% is above the water and signifies behaviour (B) which happens in an environment (E). The internal personality constitutes 90% of the iceberg. Attitudes at the first level shape behaviour. Also, beliefs and values at the second and third levels independently shape behaviour. At the final level we have the self-identity of the person which is ultimately responsible for all kinds of behaviour. More on this when we deal with Personal Effectiveness in Chapter 5 of this book.

or she or or

Thus, we can see the importance of personal values in forming attitudes.

Let us go further in understanding beliefs and values

Beliefs are statements running in our minds generated out of significant events that happened in our lives, both positive and negative. For example, if the teacher at school scolded a person and said, "You can never learn mathematics!" This gets embedded in the form of a belief that the person can never learn mathematics and continues to fare poorly. Often, this becoming a self-fulfilling prophecy. On the other hand, if the teacher says, "It's ok that you have got 40% this time, I can see that you can do very well, provided you give it some focussed attention!" This manner of speaking leads to a lasting impact on the person, and confidence builds up. In my own life, early in my career, being reprimanded for coming late to meetings - "You can never come on time!" - left a belief in me that maybe I can never be on time for any event. Today, I realise, when awareness has set in, why I used to be late in reaching airports, arriving at important meetings on time, and fulfilling a promise to the family to take them out after reaching home from the office (this happened several times), etc. Strangely enough, I also formed a condoning attitude with people in my corporate arena for coming late to work or arriving late at meetings. I can say that I have never censured anyone so far for coming late for an appointment.

Beliefs are the things we hold **true**, regardless of whether we have any proof of their objective truth. Beliefs are developed and inherited. Parents, teachers, mentors, colleagues - they all pass their beliefs on to us. We also develop beliefs resulting from personal experiences and the feelings that we associate with them in those moments. If I am consistently late, I start to believe that I am terrible at time management when, in fact, a better alarm clock and sleep habits could change that label.

A belief that one can resonate with is – if a black cat crosses your path, something untoward will happen.

There are three main types of beliefs we as humans have:

- **Beliefs about Self**

  Things such as I am smart, I am stupid, I am unlucky, I am beautiful, I am strong, etc. Beliefs about self are responsible for our motivation or demotivation. They are also known as limiting beliefs. An example of this: till recently, I had a fear of dogs because, in my early childhood, a dog chased me and almost bit me on my left forearm; it was running helter-skelter as a prankster had tied and lit a firecracker on its tail while it was sleeping.

- **Beliefs About Others**

  These beliefs are usually indoctrinated into our heads by our mentors and parents and instilled inside us by our own experiences. In this,

I may develop beliefs about my family members, bosses, peers, and subordinates and, on the social scene, beliefs about relatives, friends, and neighbours.

- **Beliefs About Life and The World:**

  Beliefs such as "life is hard," "everything is terrible," or conversely, "the world is full of possibilities," or "life is beautiful" are all beliefs we develop about the outside world. We formulate such beliefs within our domains and extrapolate them to humanity.

Now we come to Values

Values are the compass in life that tells us what is right and what is wrong.

Values are first developed in our childhood by our parents, siblings, teachers, and friends and continue to evolve as we grow older.

Values shape our behaviour. For example, if my values are honesty and perseverance, I will be honest regardless of the consequences. Perseverance means I will toil and complete the job with which I am entrusted.

There are a few key values that we believe are important in the workplace. Their corresponding behaviour is as follows:

Value	Behaviour
Respect	Respectful communication
Cooperation	Cooperating with others
Honesty	Honesty in all interactions
Fairness	Fairness in decision-making

We can summarise as follows

Our beliefs are ideas that we hold to be true. Many of these beliefs, along with our life circumstances, define our values or what is important to us in life. Our values and beliefs will determine our attitude, meaning how we treat others and ourselves and how we approach any situation. Lastly, all three determine our behaviour or how we act in given situations.

How Does Behaviour Affect Work Performance?

Workplaces can sometimes be difficult environments to navigate. One of the biggest challenges one faces is dealing with difficult co-workers and managers. Inappropriate behaviour often leads to conflicts and distractions, which can make it challenging to focus on work tasks. Additionally, undesirable behaviour can damage relationships with colleagues, making it harder to collaborate effectively.

Example:

Suppose I go to a subordinate and ask him the status of a report he was assigned to complete and hand over to me the previous day. There are two possible scenarios – The first is **when the individual has an attitude of looking at his workplace as drudgery and is bored with the work he does. This can stem from beliefs such as, "I am never appreciated at work" and "This is not what I want to do in life."** This might lead to a response - "I did not get time to do it as I was busy attending to other work you have assigned." On my asking, "When will the job get done?" the answer could be - "I will let you know in two hours' time." Thus, we can see that his behaviour manifests from a lack of commitment and a lack of compliance with commonplace agreements.

Let us now consider the second possible scenario, is **when a person looks at his work with a sense of ownership and commitment.** When I ask him about the report, the reply is - "I am just going through the finishing touches, and the report will be on your table in the next 60 minutes!" or it could be – "Sorry for the delay, however, I will complete the report and present it to you in the next two hours!" **Here, the person is driven by beliefs like "my work is my worship," "hard work helps my personal growth," "I am very lucky to have this job." etc.** This is reflected in his positive behaviour and thus affects his performance level in the organisation, as seen by his peers and bosses.

These aspects of behaviour at the workplace, at home, or in social life have been adequately dealt with in the forthcoming chapters, keeping in mind the title - 9 + 7 = 16 ways of getting Voluntary Active Support from people around us.

At a several workshops I conducted for VAS, there were people from junior and middle management levels, who reported that they get 50/60% of VAS in their organisations from people around them. However, the next question I posed was, "To what extent can we increase this VAS?" The answer was "80/90%." I then ask – "Why not 100%?" Quick comes the answer, "This is not possible." "Why?" "Because there will be instances where there is no complete understanding of what is being said or asked for and the expected results - there could probably be a mismatch between expectations and results. In addition, the basic will of the participant to execute the job will play a cardinal role."

My counter to this is:

'Whatever the mind can conceive, we can achieve' - Napoleon Hill (Think and Grow Rich).

It is better to uphold the conviction that 100% Voluntary Active Support is possible.

From another perspective, it is common knowledge that unavoidable losses can occur in certain processes. Taking the analogy of an aluminium melting furnace, we find that there is an unavoidable burning loss of approximately 3/4%, and therefore, we can consider the 96% to be 100% for calculation purposes. In the same manner, barring some unavoidable instances, 100% voluntary active support should be possible. The question then posed is - "How do you get the current level of voluntary active support you mentioned earlier?" (It would be interesting to know that I have gained a lot of insights from these questions.) I then go ahead and record on the board what the participants have to say about the different ways they get voluntary active support from people around them. It is a collection of these myriad responses that I have received over the years that have been condensed and presented as 9 + 7 = 16 ways of getting voluntary active support.

References

- *https://iulianionescu.com/blog/how-our-beliefs-and-values-shape-our-behavior/*

- *https://www.iaa.govt.nz/for-advisers/adviser-tools/ethics-toolkit/personal-beliefs-values-attitudes-and-behaviour/*

Chapter 4   The Manager – Demystified

Management has been defined in several ways by esteemed scientists in the past. Few of them are represented here.

F. W. Taylor - Management is the art of knowing what you want to do and then seeing that it is done in the best and cheapest possible manner. To manage is to forecast and plan, to organise, to command, to coordinate and to control.

Henry Fayol - Management is a social process of designing & maintaining an environment in which individuals work together in groups & efficiently accomplish selected aims.

Mary Parker Follet - Management is the art of getting things done through others.

In some training programmes I facilitated, whenever I posed the question - Who is a 'Manager?' The answers received were varied: -

- A manager is one who manages.

- A manager organises resources and controls team to achieve objectives.

- A manager is accountable for results.

- A manager takes responsibility for results.

And the list goes on. To seek an answer, we need to look at Physics wherein, by combining Boyle's Law and Charles' Law, we get the work done by a heat engine shown by the shaded area below.

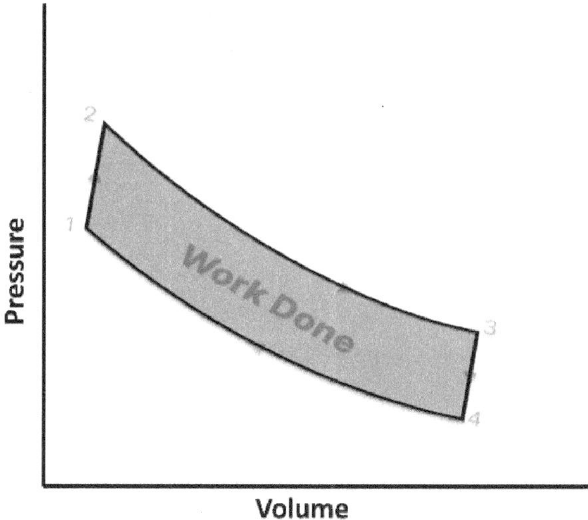

(Figure no.3: Work done by a Heat Engine)

The area inside the loop is a representation of the amount of work done during a cycle (Physics - Heat Engines). An analogy is being drawn here to depict the work done by a person.

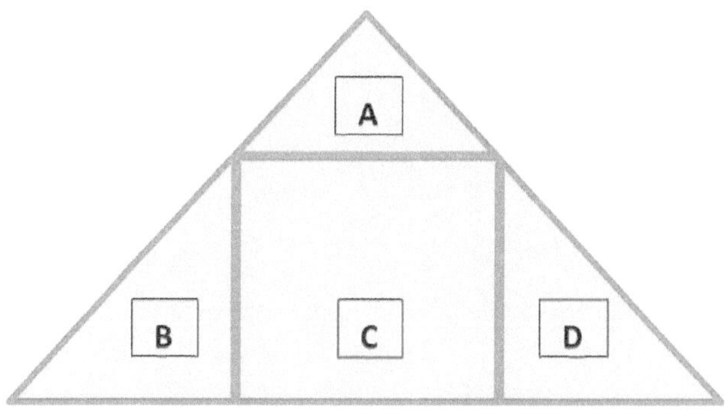

(Figure no.4: Manager defined)

Let us assume that triangle A above is the work done by a person called 'A.' He is going to be responsible and accountable for the work he is doing, i.e. area 'A.' Now, we give this person 'A' additional responsibility equal to symbolically the big red triangle. Since he will not be able to do it alone, we give him three people 'B,' 'C,' and 'D' respectively who are responsible and accountable for their corresponding areas. Now 'A' becomes responsible and accountable for *'work more than what he can do alone'* and therefore can be titled as a 'Manager.' Taking this example further, a worker on a machine is responsible and accountable for whatever happens on the machine. But he is not responsible and accountable for other workers' jobs. On the other hand, a supervisor oversees whatever happens in his shop and in a way, he gets done *more work than what he can do alone*. Often, we call this supervisor a 'Manager,' whereas a Deputy General Manager (Strategy), if working all alone and producing results is technically a non-manager. This distinction is important. It will be useful to define 'manager' in this book as, 'someone who achieves predetermined results with the voluntary active support of people around him.' The word 'around' signifies supervisors, peers, and subordinates, the person is working with. We will be using this definition of manager in explaining the principles and practice of voluntary active support throughout this book.

Chapter 5

Pre-requisites to Getting Voluntary Active Support

Before we get all excited and start aiming for VAS, some prerequisites one must be aware of.

5.1: First Pre-requisite – Getting a Handle on Personal Effectiveness

Personal effectiveness means getting the best out of oneself. It is also about how well one uses resources like energy, time, skills, strengths, etc., to achieve one's goals. In another way, personal effectiveness can be seen as the capacity to produce desired behaviours and outcomes, whether at home or work.

It is an approach to success that involves utilising all of one's energy, skill, and motivation to develop and reach the goals one sets for oneself. The key elements are: -

- Achieving personal goals.

- Development and self-awareness of strengths.

- Evaluating action plans.

Most of us know that effectiveness means 'result orientation' and personal effectiveness is the key to team effectiveness & organisational effectiveness.

Personal Effectiveness (PE) can be put in an equation form as follows:

PE = f (**K, S, A**) x (**EM**) where EM is Extrinsic Motivation, and the letters K stands for Knowledge, S for Skills, and A for Attitudes.

Knowledge can be seen in three dimensions:

a. **Domain Knowledge:** One must be reasonably familiar with his or her domain knowledge. For example – an engineer must have engineering knowledge, a doctor must have medical knowledge, a commercial person must have basic finance knowledge, and so on.

b. **Organisational Knowledge:** Knowledge of the company he or she works for. A snapshot of this comes in the induction process. However, in this VUCA world, one must very quickly learn more about the organisation – this includes services or products the company is offering, the mission, vision, goals, core values of the company, an overall sense of how work gets accomplished, including the key drivers of the business. In short - a quick and thorough understanding of the organisation and its work culture.

c. **Self-Knowledge:** Answers to questions like "How do I manage my time?" "How do I manage my stress?" "How well do I bounce back?" In summary, a personal SWOT analysis. This can be done through appropriate psychometrics and facilitation in the classroom or online.

Skill: Skill may be defined as the application of knowledge. Very often, we find that excellent domain knowledge does not necessarily result in its application. For e.g. an MBA, though proficient in knowledge, can fall short in the aspect of getting along with people and thereby restrict his application of knowledge in real-time situations. Skill thus becomes an important addition whenever we talk of Personal Effectiveness. 3 kinds of skills are imperative for an effective person:

a. **Domain Skills:** As mentioned earlier, one cannot get away with knowledge alone. Its application in work situations is paramount. In my experience, having a good superior at the initial stages accelerates this dimension of transferring domain knowledge in the form of skills at the workplace. The person who wrote the foreword for this book was instrumental as my first boss, shaping my abilities to transfer the learning of my engineering education to the shop floor very effectively. Of course, one cannot discount the willingness of the person to learn the ropes quickly. It is in the initial stages that superiors condone the mistakes that could happen while learning. The beginning of one's career and the first job could also be called the honeymoon period for one's personal learning and growth.

b. **Getting Along With People Skills:** This encompasses Communication Skills, Interpersonal Skills, etc. In essence, this skill refers to one's ability to work with peers and bosses in the initial phases and later in life with subordinates.

The crux of this book is aimed at sharpening our skills in this core area of one's life. Learning to get VAS early can help resolve many of the conflicts one faces while getting results with people.

c. **Being Proactive** – this has multiple dimensions:

Taking Initiative: Which means volunteering to take up or support any change activity when suggested by the boss. I have found that, very often, people are reluctant to put their best foot forward because they feel that their workload will increase, so why take on more responsibilities? Little do we realise that this is one cardinal factor that can lead to quicker upgradations in one's life.

One can define "**Proactivity**" as – "Creating a scenario of the future and taking a decision today for tomorrow in such a way that, if anything good is going to happen, can I advance it, and if anything, bad is going to happen, can I avert it."

In other words, being proactive is equal to foresight plus action. I have seen people having foresight but failing to act in time. To get noticed and promoted, this golden rule of always staying proactive (both on stage and off stage) can yield enormous dividends.

I have found that, in order to show one's knowledge about the subject being discussed, very often, people tend to react and say something that could be detrimental when work proceeds to the implementation stage. Instead of reacting, one must learn the art of responding, which is a considered statement or a reply after a very short reflection. This is a skill that can help us avoid any kind of conflict in the workplace, family, and social domains. It is pertinent to realise that there is a gap between stimulus and response, which can be used gainfully for answering appropriately. This ability can also keep one's anger in check.

Attitude: An attitude is the way one looks at people, events, or situations. There are three kinds of attitudes one deals with in life.

a. A positive or negative attitude towards life in general. Take the example of looking at life as a glass 'half full' or 'half empty.'

b. Attitude towards work.

Some people say - "My work is my worship," others say, "Work is boring." Still, someone else may say, "My work is my life." Thus, we can see that the attitude one has towards his or her work significantly impacts performance. Let us consider two examples.

1. The Industrial Engineer - will do a good job if he sees his work with the following mindsets.

1a. Nothing is the best. Even the best can be bettered.

1b. Whenever I see the waste of any kind, be it machine, man, material, or in the process under observation, my blood starts boiling, and I rush in to make improvements.

One can conclude that having the two attitudes shown above, will give substantial results.

2. The Materials Manager - If this person looks at materials as 'money' and not as 'shafts, tubes, or chemicals' when he/she goes on the shop floor, they see money lying all around and therefore would do his or her best to minimise inventory and take proper care of the material in terms of storage and transportation.

Thus, we can also see that the inventory carrying cost, the wastages occurring in transit, and the total inventory itself on the shop floor would be substantially minimised by the role holder.

c. Attitude towards the organisation – the way one looks at the company in which he or she is working: "This organisation belongs to me." (sense of belongingness). "If I do my job well, the company will prosper, and I will also do well in my career as time progresses."

The text above can be shown diagrammatically as follows:

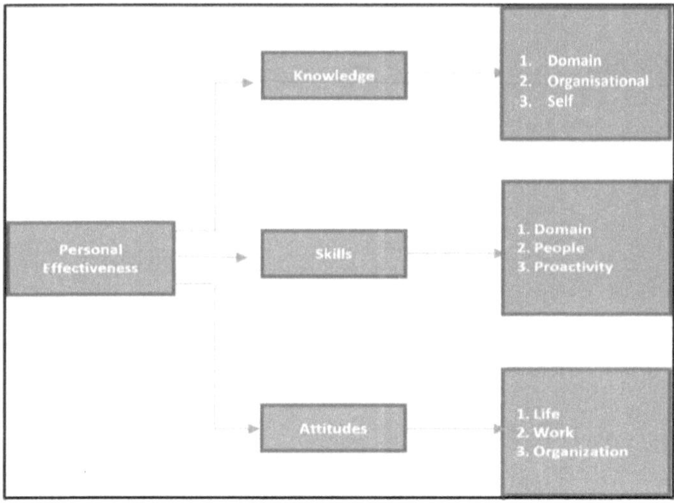

(Figure no.5: Personal Effectiveness)

References

- https://www.ipl.org/essay/The-Importance-Of-Personal-Effectiveness-P36R2W7ESCF6

5.1.a Extrinsic Motivation and its role in Personal Effectiveness

Extrinsic motivation is a type of operant conditioning, which is a form of behaviour modification. It uses rewards or punishments to increase or decrease the likelihood of specific behaviours recurring. Extrinsic motivation can be useful for persuading someone to complete a task.

Intrinsic motivation is when one engages in a behaviour because he/she finds it rewarding. One is performing an activity for its own sake rather than from the desire for some external reward. The behaviour displayed itself is its own reward.

The distinction:

Extrinsic Motivation

- Participating in a sport to win awards

- Cleaning one's room to avoid being reprimanded

- Competing in a contest to win a scholarship

- Studying because one wants to get a good grade

Intrinsic Motivation

- Participating in a sport because one finds the activity enjoyable

- Cleaning one's room because one likes a decluttered environment

- Solving a word puzzle because one finds the challenge fun and exciting

- Studying a subject one finds fun and exciting

It has been found that praise can increase internal motivation. Offering positive praise and feedback when people do something better than others can improve intrinsic motivation.

Some vital factors that can be used to increase intrinsic motivation are:

- ensuring that activities are sufficiently challenging but not impossible,

- making the activity both attention-grabbing and interesting,

- giving people personal control over how they approach the activity,

- offering recognition and praise for efforts and giving people the opportunity to compare their efforts to those of others.

Extrinsic motivation doesn't always have a tangible reward. It can also be done through non-financial means, like praise, fame, and putting employee photos in company journals with captions, etc.

In contrast, intrinsic motivation is when internal forces like personal growth or a desire to succeed fuel the drive to complete tasks. Intrinsic motivation is typically seen as a more powerful incentive for behaviours that require long-term execution.

One quote comes to my mind:

"The deepest principle of human nature is a craving to be appreciated." - William James, American Psychologist, and Philosopher.

Extrinsic motivation starts with 'acknowledgement' and is the first step in the three-part process of Extrinsic Motivation.

1st step: Acknowledgement: "I can see that you are doing a lot of hard work. I have observed you go late from office since last 3 days," is a comment made by a senior. Here, he is not saying, good job, keep it up. It is just acknowledging the fact that he has seen this person in the workplace even after office hours, and it seems he/she is doing his/her best. Just acknowledging in the mind is not enough; we must articulate the situation as things are.

Let me explain the process with an example: Years ago, while working with Crompton Greeves Limited, on the 1st of April in a particular year, I entered the office at about 8.30 a.m. I saw a group of people sitting at the first desk. They were all working. Their eyes were red and looked like they had been working all night. It was difficult to surmise whether they had gone home or slept in the office for a short time. I asked them – "Looks like you haven't slept all night." The reply was – "Sir, we dispatched 55 lorries yesterday, and it has been a record for us. We feel so proud of this achievement." I went to my cubicle and started my work. At around 11 a.m., these people came and said, "Sir, you're the only person who showed concern. So many officers have passed this way since this morning. None of them bothered to say anything to us. Maybe it is taken for granted that we are from the Excise Department, and if we worked the whole night on the last day of the year (31st March), then so what? We are paid for it. When you asked us, we felt nice hearing it," and then they went home. This is the kind of acknowledgement that helps us to get support at a time when we need it.

2nd step: Appreciation: Appreciation for good work done. Consider this story: Once, a boss, whom I knew would not tell anything to his subordinate despite the good job being done by him. I asked the person's boss, "Why don't you tell him once in a while that he's doing a good job?" The boss said, "Well, if I tell him, his performance will go down. In Hindi, there is a saying, *'Sar pe chad ke baith jaayega,'* meaning, *'he will sit on my head.'* That's the reason I don't tell him anything. Contrast this with another case where the person was not doing his job properly and instead of admonishing him, his boss kept quiet. I told the boss to give him feedback that he must pull up his socks. "No, no, Sir," said the boss. "If I reprimand him, he will even stop doing whatever work he is currently doing." There is an old saying, 'appreciate in public and reprimand in private.' However, in my experience, very often, bosses shout at a person in public, maybe out of their own need for security. The damage done to the person being shouted at is unfathomable and leaves a scar. He keeps quiet only because his job is very important to his survival. However, both appreciation and reprimand need to be given as close to the event as possible. I have seen subordinates appreciating the fact that I censured them, not in public, but on a one-to-one basis. They took it as feedback for improvement.

Genuine appreciation, when given timely, is a great motivator for people. The proverbial 'pat on the back' can do wonders to uplift the spirits of the person being appreciated. I remember a boss telling his subordinate – "Oh, that was a wonderful job you had done," and the subordinate asked him, "When, Sir?" The reply was, "Remember ten days ago when a customer was very angry and in a few minutes, you were able to calm him down? I am referring to that incident." The subordinate said, "Oh, thank you very much for that, Sir." Clearly, the effect was not the same as the boss appreciating him on the very same day or the next day. Immediacy is the key word for leveraging appreciation and reprimand. When we show appreciation to our colleagues, customers, managers, and partners, we're more likely to build trust and connect. There's a quote from Teddy Roosevelt: '*People don't care how much you know until they know how much you care.*' This sums up the essence of appreciation.

3rd step: Recognition: Recognition is all about giving a person his due in front of his peers. For example, in an MRM (Monthly Review Meeting), the boss says, "Peter, I know that you've done this job. You've got a big deal signed last week. Excellent! I am sure a lot of hard work went into making it happen. Let's give a big hand to Peter." Everybody claps. This would be termed recognition as it happens in front of a group, where the person is appreciated for his good work. Recognition, most people understand as promotions, extra incentives, or rewards. Not always so! In my mind, recognition is within a group, maybe peers, maybe bosses, maybe subordinates. If somebody is praised for good work within a group, that becomes recognition, and recognition really energises people.

References

- *https://www.healthline.com/health/extrinsic-motivation#:~:text=Extrinsic%20 motivation%20can%20be%20useful,skills%20when%20used%20in%20 moderation*

- *https://www.verywellmind.com/differences-between-extrinsic-and-intrinsic-motivation-2795384*

- *https://www.verywellmind.com/differences-between-extrinsic-and-intrinsic-motivation-2795384#citation-1*

- *https://www.verywellmind.com/differences-between-extrinsic-and-intrinsic-motivation-2795384#citation-6*

- *Tranquillo J, Stecker M. Using intrinsic and extrinsic motivation in continuing professional education.* Surg Neurol Int. 2016;7(Suppl 7):S197-9. doi:10.4103/2152-7806.179231

- *Lee W, Reeve J, Xue Y, Xiong J. Neural differences between intrinsic reasons for doing versus extrinsic reasons for doing: an fMRI study.* Neurosci Res. *2012;73(1):68-72. doi:10.1016/j.neures.2012.02.010*

- *Henderlong J, Lepper MR. The effects of praise on children's intrinsic motivation: a review and synthesis.* Psychol Bull. *2002;128(5):774-95.*

- *https://www.verywellmind.com/things-you-should-know-about-motivation-2795389#citation-4*

- *Di Domenico SI, Ryan RM. The Emerging Neuroscience of Intrinsic Motivation: A New Frontier in Self-Determination Research.* Front Hum Neurosci. *2017;11:145. doi:10.3389/fnhum.2017.00145*

5.2: Second Prerequisite - Honing Interpersonal Skills

In the business world, the term "interpersonal skills" generally refers to an employee's ability to work well with others. A lack of solid interpersonal skills can put an employee at a disadvantage where group involvement, desired assignments, positive reviews, and job advancement are concerned. Interpersonal skills are often referred to as people skills, social skills, or social intelligence. They involve reading the signals that others send and interpreting them accurately to form effective responses.

Three Pillars of Interpersonal Skills:

- Clear communication, whether you're explaining an idea or asking a question in person, in writing, or by phone.

- Attentive, careful listening.

- Confirming that you comprehend what you've heard from a colleague or customer.

In honing interpersonal skills, the following steps can be useful:

a. Having a positive mental attitude.

b. Raising one's emotional quotient.

c. Acknowledging and appreciating others' strengths.

d. Practicing mindful listening.

e. Assertive communication (neither aggressive nor passive) helps a lot.

Interpersonal skills are essential in every stage of one's life. In gaining voluntary assistance and support (VAS) from people around us, this skill becomes crucial. In fact, the support we receive is a function of

a. effective speaking (verbal communication) and b. effective listening.

5.2.a. Effective Communication and VAS

A note on effective communication:

Why learn communication skills?

There were many great people with great ideas and knowledge, but the world could not avail itself of the benefit simply because they could not convey their thoughts.

Communication skills are required throughout from womb to tomb – the power of spoken words is immense.

We need to communicate to:

- Convey ideas, information, and knowledge.

- Impart skills.

- Influence people without authority.

- Manage change.

- Manage self and others.

One of the fundamental tenets of communication is: if 'A' is talking to 'B,' 'A' gives a stimulus and 'B' gives the response, then the onus of 'B's response lies with 'A' 100%. With this tenet, one can proceed to effective communication.

5.2.b. Effective Listening and VAS

Most of us would like to think that we are good listeners. In other words, we believe that we hear what someone is saying, take it in, and interpret it correctly before responding appropriately. Unfortunately, the truth is that most of us overestimate our abilities in this area. Instead of giving the speaker our full attention, we may be formulating a reply, making a judgement about what they are saying, or even being distracted by what we're going to have for dinner. This ineffective listening leads to misunderstandings and communication breakdowns.

To get a handle on listening, it is always better to look at the difference between listening and hearing.

Listening means understanding the content at a cognitive level before giving a response.

Hearing, on the other hand, is the mechanical vibration of eardrums, which occurs even during sleep. In sleep, we hear; we don't listen. If we listen, we cannot sleep. Both cannot be done simultaneously. In normal day-to-day interactions, many of us slip into hearing mode when 'listening' to somebody or something.

I have asked this question in several groups – "When someone speaks, are you hearing or listening?" The answer I received from group members was that, in our daily lives, we hear 80% of the time and only listen 20% of the time. The remedy is to increase the 20% listening to about 60% and be aware of the **barriers to listening**.

Hearing is the act of perceiving sound and receiving sound waves or vibrations through the ear. It happens all the time – whether one likes it or not. Listening requires concentration so that the brain processes the meaning of words and sentences.

What are the barriers to listening? In my view, there are five mental barriers.

Before we delve into details, let us quickly browse through some **physical barriers** often experienced in practice:

a. Background noise – For example, several conversations happening at the same time in the office environment.

b. Feeling unwell, tired, hungry, thirsty, or needing to use the toilet frequently, too hot or too cold, leading to physical discomfort, for example, someone travelling the whole night to attend a meeting or seminar the next morning.

c. Phone communication rather than face-to-face communication allows more distractions.

d. Having a 'faraway' look may be a sign that someone is daydreaming.

e. An inappropriate posture, such as slouching, leaning back, or 'swinging' on a chair, constantly shifting posture.

However, a slightly forward bend of the listener, signifies interest in what the speaker is saying.

Here are the details of possible **mental barriers** to listening:

a. **Private Planning** is the first one. Here, we are bothered about what is happening outside the conversation domain. Let me provide an example - During a training session, one of the participants was preparing to go on leave in a few days because his brother was getting married. While the session was in progress, the participant may start thinking about the marriage function. What are the jobs to be done next in his role, how is he going to accomplish that, and so on? Now, planning involves future action. Therefore, private planning is planning about what a person is going to do and how he or she is going to do it.

    A classic example, like the one above, occurred when I was conducting a session. I found one of the participants looking at me and shaking his head, giving the impression that he was attentive to all that was being said, and it appeared that he was making notes. It was too good to be true, and I felt something was amiss. I went near him and lo and behold, found him writing his next week's tour plan.

When I asked him, "Hello, what are you doing?" he said, "Well, I have to submit this tour plan by today evening, so I'm working on it." I said, "Fine. However, you are making gestures as if you are keenly listening to me." In reply, he said, "Yes, yes, and I am sorry."

(Figure no.6: Private Planning)

Therefore, private planning involves thinking about the future while someone is speaking and becoming absorbed in that mode.

b. **Daydreaming** is the second barrier. This happens when our thoughts and attention go to the past or the future. Daydreaming can happen anywhere/anytime. It can happen when we are in conversation with someone, watching something, e.g., TV, or getting engaged in some activity. We need to be aware of it. There are only two choices – 1) Be engaged in what's happening or 2) daydream. It's one's choice to focus on the current moment, and this one develops with awareness.

Daydreaming is the thoughts that come into our minds, and it is known that in a day, we have approximately 50,000 thoughts, on an average. Thoughts are like clouds. We tend to hook on to one cloud, and that plays like a video for some time. If we don't hook on to it, it goes away. These thoughts comprise daydreaming, which we experience.

(Figure no.7: Daydreaming.)

Daydreaming is very common. It is also very natural for people to daydream. Even children can daydream in class when the teacher is speaking. Some creative thoughts and ideas are born while daydreaming. However, there is a 'time and place' element to it.

It is easy to discern when someone is daydreaming. There is a physical presence; however, mentally they are absent. Eyelids typically blink after a gap of 15 to 20 seconds. However, when someone is daydreaming, the absence of blinking is coupled with a blank stare, which is easily noticeable. During the daydreaming phase, one generally tends to stare fixatedly at a particular point for medium to long periods. The person's attention is not in the session or classroom but in their personal thoughts and dreams.

Hence, inactive listening and daydreaming can be barriers to obtaining voluntary active support.

c. **Debating** is the third barrier. Often, people debate what is being said. While they are debating within themselves, the speaker has already moved forward. They are still in debating mode, and when they become aware or wake up, they start asking questions about something that has already been covered.

(Figure no. 8: Debating.)

Debating prevents us from listening, and we go into the hearing mode. **This is another aspect that prevents us from obtaining voluntary active support.**

d. **Bias** is the next barrier that pertains to the habit of labelling people. The dictionary meaning of bias is a strong feeling of favour towards or against one group of people or one side in an argument, often not based on fair judgement or facts. For example, "This person is very lazy," or "This person is a troublemaker," "This person has anger on his nose," and so on. When we discuss about them in the same manner with peers or friends these labels get reinforced. Consequently, we find that this label turns into an attitude and shapes behavior.

We start seeing that person through a filter called 'unhelpful' or 'unsupportive.' Often, it has been seen, owing to coincidence or otherwise, that whatever happens in subsequent interactions solidifies the label that is already given to that person.

Even at home, when the spouse says something, the wife or husband will not take it seriously if the label for the wife or husband already portrays – 'A complainer' or 'Always asking for something.' Thus, the conversation does not yield results, and this can lead to loss of VAS.

(Figure no.9: Bias.)

Talking some more about bias, very often in my career, I have found that when you are already biased about the other person, there is no room for active listening. For example, I may have approached person 'Y' for help. For whatever reason, if he is not helpful, he is labelled as unsupportive. Now, this will prevent me from getting VAS from him because every time I approach him, my conversation is guarded. So, when I ask him something or when he gives some excuse or reason for not being able to provide support, I refuse to listen to the excuse because I know that this is his habit. Even though it could be a genuine reason, I don't listen, as I have already labelled him as 'unsupportive.'

Quoting Werner Erhard, (Founder of EST Training and Landmark Forum) - the words that come after 'is' - 'he is -----' or 'she is -----,' are the biggest superstitions in one's life. Like, "He is a good person," or "She is a very angry person," are mere assumptions or biases that prevent us from communicating and interacting genuinely, which, often, form the major block in getting VAS. One strategy to get out of this bias is adopting a zero-base approach. For example, when we are talking to the 'unsupportive' person, our mental approach can be – "Maybe he is 'unsupportive' or maybe he is 'supportive.' I don't know, let me find out." Coming into the present moment, we approach the person with a 'zero base' or 'zero bias.' This perspective, I have found, gives excellent results.

e. **Detouring.** What happens here is the person goes on a mental tour after listening to a 'trigger' word. I will give a practical example here. One of my subordinates asked me if he could leave early that day, as he had to take his mother to the hospital for a check-up. The word 'hospital' took me back to the time when my father was in hospital, and I was running back and forth for two weeks, interacting with the ward boys, sisters, doctors, and blood banks. All these thoughts and memories flashed by, one after the other. (Finally, Dad recovered and came back home, but that was a very traumatic experience for me.) The word 'hospital' uttered by my subordinate triggered all these thoughts. After my subordinate used the word 'hospital,' he may have said many things; however, I didn't listen to anything that he said, as I was in the past. Finally, he asked, "Sir, can I go?" I answered in the affirmative; however, I was not able to listen to a single word about what was said in between. All I remember was that he wanted to go to the hospital, but the explanation he gave, I completely missed out.

Another example of 'Detouring' will make the understanding clearer.

In one of my training sessions, a participant looked like he was physically present in the training room, but mentally, he was elsewhere.

I went to him and asked him, "Looks like you are not in this class. You have gone somewhere."

Participant: "Yes. I am not here because I have mentally gone to my village."

Me: "You have gone to your village?"

Participant: "Yes. When you used the word 'village' in your talk, I was transported to my village." (Whenever there are strong experiences related to a word, one tends to go into that space in an instant.)

Me: "What did you see in your village?"

Participant: "I will be visiting my village next month. The last time I went there, I planted four coconut trees. I want to see how much they have grown and how many have been eaten up by animals or destroyed."

Me (I get a bit angry and ask him): "Well, then you must have gone to the well to see how much water is there."

Participant: "I was about to go when you called out to me, and I woke up." (He became aware of the surroundings.)

(Figure no. 10: Detouring.)

This is known as detouring – which is going on tour at the mention of a 'trigger' word. Most of us experience these kinds of triggers. All our experiences are stored somewhere in our consciousness. Experiences that are strong and deep in nature are stacked at the bottom of the deck and as they become less and less intense, they rise to the top. Peripheral experiences will not emerge so quickly, but very deep experiences will come out when we hear some trigger words or even when we sense some cues like a particular scene, particular smell, and particular touch and feel connected to that experience. **Thus, we miss out on listening, and consequently, our VAS is affected.**

We have just seen five barriers that prevent us from listening. To get voluntary active support, the aspect of Effective Listening is very crucial. We can consider effective speaking as the other side of the coin. We shall consider this in the next section. Listening is an important leadership skill because it contributes to employee engagement. Employees who feel like their perspective matters share information openly and candidly which can be invaluable in effective problem-solving and timely goal accomplishment for both individuals and teams. Being present and listening to what others have to say takes patience and practice, especially if we are conscious and aware of the barriers to listening. Recognising and working to overcome the barriers improves the quality of leadership, increases positive results, and leads to a more engaged and productive workforce.

Additional Note:

To listen effectively, one could practice reflecting. Reflecting involves paraphrasing back to the speaker with the emotion about what they have said in a manner like, "Looks like you are angry." or "It sounds frustrating that this happened to you."

5.2.c. Effective Speaking and VAS

Effective speaking means, being able to say what one wants to say, in such a way, that it is heard and acted upon.

In a world dominated by technology and rapid-fire messaging systems, the skill of effective speaking is more important than ever. Our attention spans are short, and our words are few, so being able to communicate effectively is vital.

Effective speaking is not just about saying what you mean. It is speaking so that your message is understood and motivating. You can accomplish both through your word choice and the style and tone of your message.

- **Clarity:** The first aspect of effective speaking is clear articulation. Clarity comes from preparing ourselves well for communication. If I must talk to my subordinate and give him a project, then I must be well-prepared with information about the project. Only then can I narrate the context and the content to him or her. Preparation will also help in answering any questions related to the project when put forward by my subordinate before he/she takes on the task. This, in turn, will help me gain VAS from him/her because he/she has fully understood what is required of him/her. Preparation is crucial in dealing with any stakeholder, be it a vendor, customer, boss, or peer. The tagline is clarity. **Clarity in communication comes with preparation.**

- **Body language and gestures** come next, which emanate from the enthusiasm one has towards the work he or she engages in. Staying motivated and enthused from within will cause appropriate body language. One cannot be taught how to move the body or show certain gestures while speaking. The answer lies in maintaining a certain level of intrinsic motivation – how can one do that?

For instance, I loved playing cricket in my younger days, and often on Sundays our team would get together and play on the ground with a tennis ball and be engaged there from early morning till 3 p.m. with a meagre breakfast and some soft drinks in tow. The engagement level used to be so high that a late lunch was of no concern. Here, passion takes over. However, while doing a project at work, the same kind of enthusiasm is not seen probably because, work is not in line with one's passion.

There are only two choices; one - given a choice, for full energy, enthusiasm, and engagement, **do the work we love** OR two - if there is no choice, **we love the work that we do**. The first one seems to be the ideal choice. However, life does not present only those jobs or work that we are fond of doing and therefore we must learn to take the other choice quickly and get started. In my own experience, the first choice above is a reality for 20-25% of the time. Further in this choice, there is passion. From passion comes enthusiasm and from enthusiasm emerges body language naturally. **It comes from within.**

Often, I have found it necessary to gauge this aspect in my subordinates and peers. Whatever they are saying or doing, is it out of passion and enthusiasm, or just out of the need to complete the job or gain more time for finishing a deadline?

- **Eye contact** is the third point. With eye contact comes the message that you are important to me, and I care and have respect for you. VAS depends very much on the person connected. If I am talking to Mr. Z, or maybe four or five people together, like a team meeting, I can focus my eyes on the person to whom I am speaking and occasionally also look at the others. Doing so, I am completely with the group. Involving everyone with appropriate eye contact is very important for getting VAS from groups.

- **Modulating pitch, voice and tone** is the fourth item to manage the environment in a better way. For example, if we speak in a monotone, it makes listeners sleepy. A classic example is the lullaby sung by mothers for their children. A close examination will reveal that lullabies are mostly sung in a monotone. This makes the child sleepy. People don't enjoy listening to us when we speak in a monotone way. We must flex our voice in a way that there are ups and downs in the tone and quality of the voice. It facilitates active listening from people we are talking to.

- **Getting instant feedback** is the fifth and final one. As we converse with people, getting a handle on how the other person is feeling is important. One can quickly realise that the listener is bored or very much interested because the giveaway is their body language. The importance of learning body language signals is mandatory to understand the actions and reactions seen in the person.

(Few instances of reading a person's body language are reproduced here).

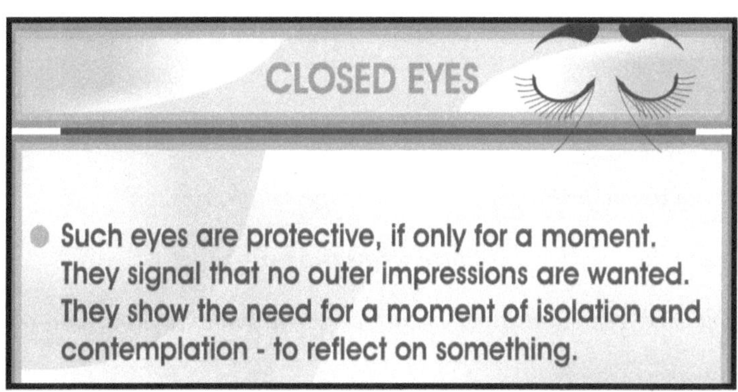

THE DIRECT LOOK

- With eyes open wide and looking directly at the person being spoken or listened to, this signals spontaneous undivided attention to others.

THE LOOK FROM ABOVE

- To look at somebody from above is the classical expression of superiority.

- The head is drawn back signifying critical distance.

OPEN HANDS

- Those presenting their arguments by showing the palms or their hands are signalling that they trust others and are interested in their opinion.

References

- https://www.investopedia.com/terms/i/interpersonal-skills.asp

- https://www.listeningears.in/difference-hearing-listening/

- https://www.indeed.com/career-advice/career-development/overcome-listening-barriers

- https://www.skillsyouneed.com/ips/effective-speaking.html#:~:text=Effective%20 speaking%20means%20being%20able,be%20able%20to%20speak%20 effectively

5.3: Third Pre-requisite - An Experience of Trust & Commitment

Trust, respect, and effective communication are three essential elements for building quality relationships in the workplace. Relationships are built over time when one person has respect for another. Gradually, trust begins to pervade throughout the organisation as well; however, trust-building is a relatively slow and long process compared to other business processes. The good news is that it can be accelerated with open interaction and good communication skills. Building trust among top-performing teams has much to do with increasing communication skills and ensuring that everyone feels valued.

While many believe that trust is created by grand gestures in a relationship, research highlights that trust is built in small, seemingly insignificant moments. These are the moments that demonstrate your commitment to your boss, subordinate, or peer.

Trust and faith are marginally different in sense and meaning. Trust can be seen as an unconditional belief in a person, whereas, faith refers to the confidence in the abilities/competencies of a person. While delegating some work, we generally do so by the faith we have in the person. However, it is the trust factor that is responsible for getting excellent results. Trust is built reciprocally. First, I trust a person and when he or she experiences that, they reciprocate the trust. **An atmosphere of trust in the organisation is a great booster for getting VAS from people.**

Commitment is different from a promise. Transforming promises into reality determines the true character and dedication of a person. Much depends on the promises we make to our fellow workers, our clients and ourselves. Making promises and converting them into reality is serious business. In business, making promises or carrying the ball is seldom sufficient. We must accomplish goals and go further in the achievement of stated outcomes. In other words, a promise can be broken, or a re-promise can be made. However, commitment once made needs to be adhered to, although there could be rare occasions of re-commitment in the face of uncontrollable extraneous circumstances. In commitment, actions speak louder than words. Actions to support words require more than creativity and rhetoric. It requires discipline and sacrifice. It is only by our actions that we generate results and achieve lasting recognition. One element that comes in between fulfilling commitment is 'procrastination,' which goes with the frequent excuse, "I have no time" or "I am running short of time." However, when we use the word commitment, it is making time when there is none. Time is an elusive commodity. It is the dimension in which action takes place, and all the work gets done. I have found in my experience that most people have integrity and do live up to expectations. We often jump to the conclusion that there is some catch in the suggestions made by people, peers, or superiors. We must spend our energy accomplishing tasks rather than second-guessing each other.

References

- *https://www.ellevatenetwork.com/articles/7406-building-trust-and-commitment-in-the-workplace*

- *https://opus.lib.uts.edu.au/bitstream/10453/2188/3/2006015067.pdf*

- *https://www.betterup.com/blog/how-to-build-trust --- In abeyance*

- *https://www.kylebenson.net/relationship-trust-commitment/*

5.4: Fourth Pre-requisite - Basic Conflict Resolution Skills

Conflict is a natural part of any workplace, especially in those with many people of varying responsibilities and personalities who work together. It is important to manage conflicts so that the workplace can continue to be a positive and collaborative environment where employees are happy and productive.

Conflict resolution is the process of resolving disagreements and coming up with solutions that are mutually agreeable to multiple parties, allowing two or more parties to reach a peaceful resolution to a dispute. Conflict resolution skills are useful in nearly every job and industry.

It is often observed that in the workplace:

- Conflict may occur between co-workers, supervisors, and subordinates, or between service providers and their clients or customers.

- Conflict can also arise between groups, such as management and the labour force, or between entire departments.

- Team conflicts arise when there are disagreements over the goals, methods, or needs of the team.

The principles enumerated in this book, 9 + 7 = 16 ways of getting VAS from people can come in handy in situations of conflict and allow team members to understand each other better, creating smoother working relationships in the future.

Kenneth W. Thomas and Ralph H. Kilmann, researchers, conflict pioneers, and authors, have clearly mentioned five types of conflict resolution modes, which are shown in the diagram below:

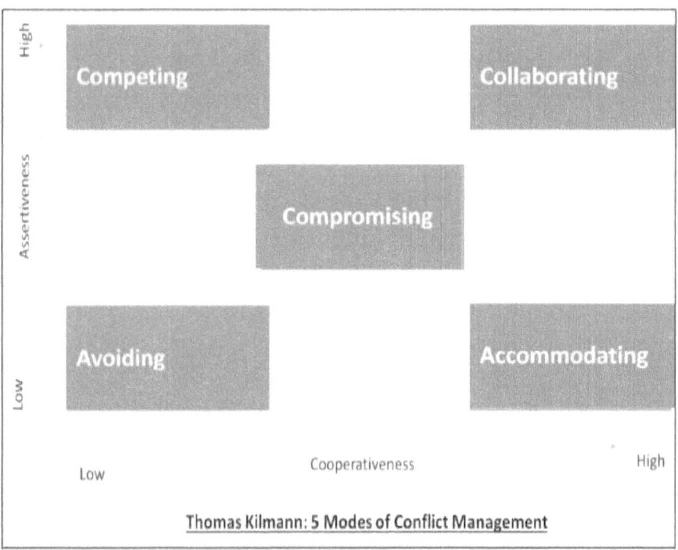

(Figure no.11: Thomas Kilmann: 5 modes of Conflict Management)

Source-https://www.researchgate.net/figure/Thomas-Kilmann-Conflict-Mode-Instrument

Out of the five modes described in the diagram, the first quadrant is low in sensitivity to the other person and low in courage, referred to as self. In the avoidant conflict management style, there is 'dodging' the issue until it resolves itself, pushing the problem off into the future or altogether ignoring the issue.

The second quadrant on the below right in the diagram pertains to accommodation and happens when the sensitivity or feelings for the other person are more than the courage required for a constructive confrontation. In the accommodating conflict management style, we put aside our priorities and focus on others.

Competition sets in when courage in self is far more than the feeling for the other person. This is a win-lose situation. When we choose to use this conflict management style, we take a firm stance with a mindset of getting what we want. While his conflict management style solves disputes quickly, it may come off as an authoritarian style that suppresses ideas, concerns, and feedback.

In getting VAS from people, a high courage and a high sensitivity towards others' feelings will carry the day. Compromise is a mild win-win, wherein we aim to partially satisfy people on both sides of the conflict. However, both parties leave the table partly dissatisfied. One side might feel they've compromised too much and the other thinks that they could have easily got more than what was offered to them in the bargain.

In other words, it is win + win/2, essentially because there is a residual feeling of dissatisfaction on both sides at the end of the compromise. For example, if I was expecting five lakhs from a person for damages incurred during the execution of a contract and a settlement is made for four lakhs as a compromise, neither of us would be happy. If you were to ask me, I would probably say, "I would have got more if I had persisted." The other party would reciprocate, "Four lakhs is too much. I think just three lakhs would have been enough. I have paid more than required." This is what could happen in most compromised situations.

In the arena of getting VAS, we must aim towards the desirable strategy of collaboration. Here, we get a pure win-win. How does that happen? Collaborating is a combination of being assertive and cooperative.

Embracing this style means we aim for a 'win-win' situation. We will work with others to find a solution that fully satisfies everyone and minimises negative feelings. Very often this mode can give us the third alternative solution, not considered either by party 'A' or party 'B.'

Three imperative pointers:

i. Appreciating the others' point of view and not reacting on impulse.

ii. Put forward views in a clear-cut manner – (refer to the 2nd pre-requisite above – Effective Speaking, pg. no. 47)

iii. Be open to the possibility of a third view emerging, which is neither my view nor the other person's view.

Hence, it is suggested to go in for collaboration, as much as possible, for effective VAS.

Compromise is the 'last resort' action, to be used only when collaboration has failed or only when there is no other alternative. Let us remember that collaboration is a strong win-win resulting from both parties willingly working together to find an agreeable solution.

Let's have an example here. One of my subordinates wanted to take leave on a particular day to attend his cousin's wedding. It clashed with the day our company president was visiting us and he was going to review some of our projects. This day was important for our department. It was therefore important for me to convince my subordinate to stay back.

Well! It was a sensitive issue. After all, there was a wedding in his family and emotions were involved. The drawback was - if I directly asked him to stay back, he wouldn't do so. He would say the wedding was very important and that such occasions expect family members to be present, and so on. It was important to make him see the severity of the situation and what was at stake.

I decided to use a softer approach. I engaged in a dialogue with him. I told him, "You have two choices. If you are here when the president comes, you will be able to explain the project to him in your own words, since this project is your baby. You are the one who implemented the project hence you should get visibility. But if you go, I must take somebody else, but that would be the second choice. You will lose the opportunity to meet the president, and you know he comes only once a year to look at how things are going on in our lab. It's your choice. You must decide. If you stay it's fine, if you don't, that's also fine. But remember, you will lose out on this opportunity which could have immense value for you and your career.

The way I put it across to him, "What's in it for you?" he immediately decided to stay back. He said he would go the previous night, attend the early morning marriage rituals, and come to the lab by 2 p.m., before the president arrived. Thus, this outcome was a win-win situation for both sides. Clearly articulating the consequences in decision-making can help us get VAS.

Consequential decision-making, as we call it, is not about winning an argument but finding the best solution, with a clear purpose and intent. When this happens, the experience of trust and commitment gets enhanced (refer to the 3rd pre-requisite, page no. 51).

References

- *https://kilmanndiagnostics.com/overview-thomas-kilmann-conflict-mode-instrument-tki/)*

- *https://matterapp.com/blog/5-conflict-management-styles-to-improve-your-productivity*

5.5: Fifth Pre-requisite - Locus of Control and Its Implications for VAS

The concept was developed by Julian B. Rotter in 1954 and has since become an aspect of personality psychology. Locus of Control refers to the extent to which individuals believe that they can control events that affect them. Individuals with high internal control believe that events result primarily from their own behaviour and actions. Those with a high external locus of control believe that powerful factors like fate or chance determine events in their lives.

(Figure no. 12: Locus of Control)

For example, if a person with an internal locus of control passes or fails in an interview, he will praise or blame himself and his abilities, whereas a person with a strong external locus of control will tend to praise or blame external factors such as the HR, his luck, or the environment. J. B. Rotter (1975) also cautioned that internality and externality represent two ends of a continuum, not an either-or typology.

In my experience, people who get regular VAS from others tend to have a higher internal locus of control. Some empirical validation of the above is available in a paper by Locke (1969). Job satisfaction is the function of the perceived relationship between what one wants from one's job and what he or she gets. Several variables may affect the feeling of satisfaction at the workplace, such as work, family, conflict, injustice, perception, social support, immediate changes in personal-professional life, work culture, stress, and locus of control. Among these variables, stress and locus of control are the most important and frequent predators of job satisfaction. My interpretation from experience – (this is a hypothesis and untested) – is that **people with a high locus of control will have a sense of more control over the environment and the results that they get, and therefore, that person will be able to get substantially more VAS from people.**

Individuals with an internal locus of control are more likely to acquire greater work resources compared to people with an external locus of control. They are good with relationship building and are loyal to colleagues and their organisation. These are some of the reasons why their colleagues, peers, and bosses are more willing to support them when the need arises.

"An internal locus of control emerges when we develop a mental habit of transforming chores into meaningful choices, when we assert, that we have authority over our lives." **- Charles Duhigg**

While discussing VAS, it would be helpful to look at one more concept called self-efficacy. The term 'self-efficacy' was first coined by Albert Bandura (1977), a Canadian American psychologist and a professor at Stanford University. Albert Bandura has defined self-efficacy as people's beliefs in their capabilities to exercise control over their own functioning and over events that affect their lives. One's sense of self-efficacy can provide the foundation for motivation, well-being, and personal accomplishment. People's beliefs in their efficacy are developed by four main sources of influence, including:

i. Mastery experiences (expectations surpassed performance)

ii. Vicarious (indirect) experiences

iii. Social persuasion

iv. Emotional states

High self-efficacy has been linked to with numerous benefits to daily life, such as resilience to adversity and stress, healthy lifestyle habits, improved employee performance, and educational achievement. **People who have a high sense of self-efficacy bounce back from failure; they approach things in terms of how to manage them rather than worrying about what can go wrong. They are solution-oriented and confident about themselves and their decisions, hence able to get sustained VAS from people around them willingly.**

Relationship of stress, locus of control, and self-efficacy: Self-efficacy can be something that people use to deal with the stress that they are faced with in their everyday lives. Some findings suggest that higher levels of external locus of control combined with lower levels of self-efficacy are related to higher illness-related psychological distress. People who report a more external locus of control also report more concurrent and future stressful experiences and higher levels of psychological and physical problems. These people are also more vulnerable to external influences and as a result, they become more responsive to stress.

References

- *https://en.wikipedia.org/wiki/Locus_of_control*

- *https://www.simplypsychology.org/self-efficacy.html*

Categorised list of 9+7 = 16 Ways of getting Voluntary Active Support

Chapter 6

Getting Voluntary Active Support from People – Part I

Having completed the prerequisites, let us proceed to the intended outcome of this book: namely, 9 + 7 = 16 ways of obtaining voluntary active support from people. For ease of recall and practical usage, I have divided the 9 + 7 = 16 ways into four parts, namely:

1. MANAGING SELF

1.1: Playing a Supportive Role

A supportive work environment is one where job performance and emotional, physical, and mental well-being are valued. Supportive workplaces are attuned to 'sensitive' matters that might make employees feel uncomfortable or less than their best selves (race, gender, caste, etc.). A team approach means everyone is working toward a shared goal.

The benefits of supporting others in the workplace are extremely large. Specifically, when employees assist others, it allows them to achieve benefits such as positively influencing workplace culture, developing leadership skills, and further strengthening trust within the workplace. Supporters will gain satisfaction from being able to assist those who need help within the business.

In today's dramatically reconfigured world, success is increasingly dependent on how we interact with others. Adam Grant, an award-winning researcher and Wharton's highest-rated professor, has examined the surprising forces that explain why some people rise to the top of the success ladder while others remain at the bottom or in the middle. He has effectively detailed how playing a supporting role and supporting others could benefit us in ascending to the top echelons of the hierarchy.

Playing a supportive role is essential, and the best analogy that can be drawn is from the Festival of Janmashtami in India (as shown in the figure). The celebrations include breaking the '*Dahi Handi*,' in other words, breaking the earthen pot filled with curd and other goodies, tied up at a height, sometimes equal to 1 or 2 floors.

(Figure no. 13: Playing a Supportive Role)

To achieve this, groups of enthusiasts called *Govindas*, which literally means Lord Krishna and his friends, take their turn in forming a pyramid and culminate in breaking the pot and sharing the goodies among themselves.

In the above pyramid formation, even if one person attempts to move out of the pyramid, the entire structure collapses like a deck of cards. Not one person in this pyramid can let go. This is how one should see oneself in the whole pyramid of events or processes and not think that the role they play is small or big or of no consequence. Every role is important. We must look at the bigger picture. The understanding that I'm playing a supportive but important role must be ingrained. If I move away or don't give support to people, then it's likely the whole system may not survive. **It is just the mindset that playing a supportive role is important, which in turn can generate substantial VAS for oneself.**

References

- *https://www.employeeconnect.com/blog/7-benefits-supporting-others-work/*

- *Supportive Leadership - Learn How to Be a Supportive Leader (corporatefinanceinstitute. com)*

1.2: Be True To Self

"To thine own self be true" …. William Shakespeare

When one is true to oneself, the person is completely honest with his/ her feelings, values, and desires. It also means communicating feelings wholeheartedly both with oneself and others, allowing truth to flow into the world.

(Figure no.14: Be True to Self)

By doing this, I have found that I become vulnerable and more humane, and this often generates VAS through enhanced camaraderie.

Another perspective - A glimpse of this is found in the Johari Window, specifically in Quadrant no. II, often referred to as the **'Secret Quadrant,'** which encompasses **'I know, but others don't know'**. This is where we often behave through facades, leading to negative consequences. For instance, if we fail to disclose certain important facts during an interview, and the same situations arises later, wherein we are unable to perform as expected.

For example, for the post of an Industrial Relations Officer interview, one candidate (who was later hired and put on probation) told me that he was very good at Industrial Relations. When questioned about handling lockouts and strikes, he categorically said he knew all about it and had handled many tough situations in his previous jobs. However, within three months, a conflict situation arose in the company, wherein two unions were having an inter-union rivalry issue, there was violence on the campus, and lo and behold, this person was conspicuously missing. Efforts to contact him proved futile. Later at night, when things died down and the situation was somehow managed, the top cabinet came together to discuss the future turn of events. At that time, this person suddenly surfaced. When asked about his whereabouts, he said he was at the godown, canteen, shop floor, etc., where some people were getting beaten up, and he tried hard to stop one group from injuring the other.

It was very clear that this was an excuse, and he was not willing to come and take the situation head-on. He didn't have the experience to do so, even though he mentioned it in the interview. Due to this, the end result was that he was asked to look for some other employment once his probation period was over. Moral of the story - if we hide crucial information from others, sooner or later, it will surface and create avoidable negative consequences.

Let us examine one more case in point. Often, in senior-level interviews, a question is asked, "What are your values?' Most people reply - honesty, integrity and so on. When we ask for evidence – "tell us a time when a particular value was demonstrated", examples do not come so easily. This means that the person is not able to substantiate whatever he is claiming.

Being true to oneself consistently gives us ample VAS. In difficult situations, in negotiating with unions, I was fortunate to get the leeway to bring about peaceful conclusions, specifically when the unions do not see eye to eye with the management.

Telling someone that we are simply "fine" when we are not, does a great disservice to the ensuing interactions. Being true to oneself entails embracing all aspects of one's existence.

Being vulnerable will help us understand which type of people we can most relate to. We have all made the mistake of sharing something personal with someone we should not have, only to end up hurt due to backstabbing or betrayal. It is good to love all people without question, but it is best to place total faith in true friends who are worthy of trust.

References

- *https://www.mindbodygreen.com/0-3617/The-Importance-of-Being-True-to-Yourself.html*

- *https://www.lifehack.org/articles/communication/10-reasons-true-yourself.html*

- *https://www.essentiallifeskills.net/betruetoyourself.html - from facebook*

- *https://www.researchgate.net/publication/286980630_Organisational_culture_A_study_of_selected_organisations_in_the_manufacturing_sector_in_the_NCR)*

- *https://www.thebalancecareers.com/how-to-walk-your-talk-1916726*

1.3: Openness and Frankness

As nouns, the difference between openness and frankness is that openness is an accommodating attitude or opinion, as in, receptivity to new ideas, behaviours, cultures, peoples, environments, experiences, etc., while frankness is the plainness of speech, candour, and honesty.

Openness refers to being open to criticism and feedback. Frankness, on the other hand, is the ability to speak one's mind and not unduly care about others' presence or opinions. Let us examine these two facets in detail by referring to the first two letters of the 'OCTAPACE' culture propounded by Professors T.V. Rao and Udai Pareek. (O stands for Openness and C stands for (positive) Confrontation). The remaining letters stand for – Trust, Autonomy, Proactivity, Authenticity, Collaboration and Experimentation.

Here, we will take an example from the performance appraisal feedback situation. When my boss tells me that I am not good at teamwork, the first thing is to examine the statement in more detail rather than outright reacting and negating what was being said. Usually, the reaction is "no, no, Sir, I am quite good at teamwork – there has been a mistake." This will lead to arguments and not lead us anywhere. On the other hand, if I can positively confront my boss and ask for more details as to how he has concluded this and can he give few examples? This interaction now takes a different turn and instead of a possible intense argument, paves the way for a better understanding. This stance taken by my me, in a way, has enabled both of us to get substantial VAS from each other in future.

In the above example, 'frankness' refers to the ease with which my boss told me about three instances he had observed, wherein I lacked teamwork. Being frank is also a measure of the courage of an individual – this comes with a caveat that whatever is being said must be, 1) the truth experienced by the person giving the feedback, 2) the events indicated are as close to the appraisal as possible, and 3) stated objectively without any bias. Frankness includes being sensitive to the listener.

(Figure no.15: Openness and Frankness)

In another example, when a suggestion was given to me on the shop floor, that the lathe could be run at a faster speed and the depth of cut simultaneously increased. This suggestion came from the operating mechanic. I was the Production Engineer concerned. Without bringing ego into the picture, I said let us think over it and work on it. This would be 'openness.' Almost immediately, I asked him to do few tests and verify.

It was found that the surface finish was not satisfactory and not within acceptable limits. So, logically, the suggestions given could not be taken forward. However, it opened the pathway to another kind of tool tip being tried out. We started using carbide tips, which, at a higher speed, gave a very good surface finish.

By deploying openness and taking positive action without outright rejection of the idea, I was able to generate VAS from the entire section.

1.4: Setting Examples to Motivate People

There is nothing more powerful for employees than observing the "big bosses" perform the actions or behaviours they are advocating. As Mahatma Gandhi once said - "Be the change you wish to see in the world."

It is expected that employees will follow rules when rule makers comply with the rules themselves.

(Figure no.16: Setting examples to motivate people)

It is also helpful for the higher-ups to get involved occasionally in the actual operations or at least make deeper inquiries about the actual work being done. People will trust the leadership who can roll up their sleeves.

Senior managers can take the help of peer feedback on walking their talk. It is difficult for subordinates to point out inconsistencies. Confronting a manager takes courage, therefore it is recommended that senior managers be accountable to each other for their own behaviour.

Going further, as a leader, if I expect that people should come on time, what I must do is, come on time myself first. It all boils down to complete alignment in what we think, what we say and what we do. This generates trust and consequently we get VAS from the people whom we lead.

Another example a leader can set is the submission of reports on time. Assume for a moment that I must commence a team meeting – it will be useful to declare how I had kept the commitment to my seniors the previous day, and that I worked the whole night to complete the presentation and reports for the board meeting today at 9.30 a.m. This result-orientation, perseverance, and compliance with deadlines can be seen by teammates and this sets the right context for getting voluntary active support.

People learn by observing behaviours rather than listening to sermons. Setting examples to motivate people is very important, and includes the way we ask empowering questions. For example, we ask this question – 'This is the problem we are facing now! Any suggestions for its mitigation?' Normally silence follows. After a couple of minutes, we start a round-robin' on what people have to say and thus a brainstorming session starts. Ideas can be noted down on the black/whiteboard and the meeting then progresses with each one participating.

People tend to believe what they see, and half of what they hear. I have often seen that, though we want to be role models, many times we give knowledge or lecture the people on the dos and don'ts. Only lecturing has negligible effect. When we show people that we walk the talk, they get motivated to do the same.

Reference

- *https://study.com/academy/lesson/the-managers-role-in-providing-a-supportive-work-environment.html*

Chapter 7

Getting Voluntary Active Support from People – Part II

2. MANAGING OTHERS

2.1: More Direct Interactions

(Figure no.17: More Direct Interactions)

In this digital age, we tend to communicate with direct reportees via email, instant messaging, phone, and text. A face-to-face, one-on-one meeting, according to Elizabeth Grace Saunders, the author of How to Invest Your Time Like Money, and the founder of Real-Life E Time Coaching & Training, undoubtedly is an important productivity tool we have as a manager.

No doubt, when there are technical details involved, images or figure work, one must use other appropriate means of communication. When it comes to briefings about work to be done, it is better to communicate personally on a one-to-one or many, what work is to be done and how, and follow it up with a mail for record and follow-up purposes.

There are three reasons why these open interactions with team members are beneficial:

1. They are closer to the point of action and the team members have a better comprehension of what is happening – this factor can be missed while answering an email.

2. The team members have a better understanding of the working environment and are in a position often, to spot possible or potential conflicts. These inputs are extremely useful in decision-making.

3. Through direct interactions we come to know the personal preferences of the team members, and this hugely helps in the delegation of work. This enhances productivity and employee satisfaction.

When we are talking to someone, emotions are involved and invested. If there is any friction, sparks will fly. The sparks, which fly in the air, get extinguished. However, when there is a covert feeling of resistance to what is being said and the same is not expressed, it is akin to the sparks going under the carpet. These sparks slowly burn the carpet, sometimes to ashes and we are not even aware. It is best to keep sparks in the air and not under the carpet. Expressing points of view and associated emotions is better than repressing them.

Talking to people, notice their reaction to what is being said, and then, if there are any issues, see what can be done to sort things out is the best option. Later, it would be prudent to record notes of discussions in a subsequent email. The point is, that as far as possible, we must try and have face-to-face communications, more direct interactions, to help eliminate any misunderstandings that could happen and provide clarity to both sides in the conversation. When any communication requires confirmation, for example, the outcome of a project, analysis or report, then email is necessary.

Supporting behaviours include:

1. Open and honest communication.

2. Maintaining a positive and friendly attitude.

3. Encouraging feedback.

Another helpful practice would be to openly declare how much time a person can expect a response to an email. I remember my group president saying – Any employee who writes to me can expect a reply in 48 hours. I have observed that following this method has benefited me in terms of getting VAS from people around me.

References

- *https://www.indeed.com/career-advice/career-development/communicating-effectively-with-employees*

- *https://ivypanda.com/essays/managerial-direct-interaction-with-employees/*

- *Hummer, D. A. (2016). Organizational climate and culture: An introduction to theory, research, and practice. Human Resource Development Quarterly, 27(2), 297-301.*

- *https://hbr.org/2016/08/how-to-make-your-one-on-ones-with-employees-more-productive*

2.2: Be True to Others

Simply put, this is not talking to others through masks or facades. This does not mean that we become diplomatic and hide something or manipulate people. In my experience, authentic communication usually gets quick results.

(Figure no.18: Be true to others)

However, the skill lies in managing the negative energy the other person may be venting. I have used terms like "What you are saying might be true, however let's look at it from a different perspective." Whenever I found the time not right for forging a closure, I asked for another appointment with the same person and took up the same issue in a different setting; of course, the context remained the same. The intervening time gives both parties a chance to get ideas and hammer out a solution.

Being authentic makes life easier. From an individual's perspective, being authentic requires one to accept both strengths and weaknesses. From a group's perspective, being authentic is not just about showing your personality to the world, it is about accepting and respecting other people's personalities too. Being authentic is more about being honest to one's inner world than the outer world.

There are few pointers to be authentic when we are dealing with others. It may sound difficult, however, the practice of following behaviours, over a while, can become one's second nature. Here I would like to define authenticity as "complete alignment to what one thinks, says and does

(In Sanskrit we say Manasa, Vaacha and Karmana – Thought, Word and Deed)"

a. Not to lie – Occasionally we often become people pleasers and suppress the truth. This is the hard part; however, one needs to realise that we become happier and healthier when we live our truth.

b. Keeping quiet and not speaking is not the answer to the avoidance of lies. For example, when someone is doing something that feels wrong to me, I need not stay silent. Instead, I can tell them/him/her the truth: "I feel nervous and upset when you are doing that. It is not the right thing for me, and I do not feel right about staying silent in this situation." One quote comes to my mind - "What is true for us tends to make us feel stronger and freer. On the other hand, lies tend to feel like constraint and constriction." - Christine Carter.

c. Loving and accepting oneself, with all the flaws, anger, fear, sadness, and pettiness, is in the end, the only thing that enables one to be authentic. It is also the greatest gift one can give to self. No wonder, it is the reason why authenticity makes us happier and healthier and connected to those around us.

I have often found difficulty in being authentic in a conference room when the boss suggests an idea and looks around the table for views and validation. Very often, I am not convinced to say, "Yes, yes, the idea is good," but in the end, I prefer to be true to myself and have resorted to the following statement - "Sir, prima facie, the idea looks okay. However, I have some reservations, which need to be examined, and I need time for the same. Maybe I can meet you in your cabin in the evening for a few minutes and state my point of view."

Even among friends and associates, we never mean the truth or reality when we say - 'I will join you in 5 minutes. Often, those 5 minutes get stretched to 10 and 15, leading to heartburn. I have often found that people can take the truth and manage if I tell them that it will take 30 minutes for me to join you.

This lessens the pressure on both sides and the trust factor increases. When we are authentic, **VAS is more or less guaranteed**.

Reference

- https://greatergood.berkeley.edu/article/item/five_ways_to_be_fully_authentic

2.3: Immediate Appreciation

Another powerful way to get Voluntary Active Support is immediate appreciation and immediate reprimand. Very often this aspect skips our attention.

(Figure no.19: Immediate appreciation)

Appreciation generally means "recognition and enjoyment of the good qualities of someone or something." In the workplace, appreciation can be as simple as saying "thank you" for a job well done, for completing a project quickly, or for coming to a meeting prepared and ahead of time. Appreciation improves workplace morale. Showing appreciation to an employee creates a ripple effect in the workplace. An employee who feels appreciated is highly likely to show appreciation to their co-workers and other team members. Appreciation is a powerful everyday tool that managers and leaders can use with their team. Unfortunately, it is underutilised and many managers that I have worked with say, "Why should I say thank you and appreciate someone who is just doing the job they are paid for?"

"The powerful motivator in our lives isn't money; it's the opportunity to learn, grow in responsibilities, contribute to others, and be recognised for achievements." – Frederick Herzberg, Psychologist.

Three cardinal principles of appreciation:

a. Do not fake it – This refers to praising someone for a hidden purpose. Being genuine will help.

b. Go across boundaries – to subordinates, peers and even bosses. It can be extended to home, as well as social life.

c. Keep appreciation timely – Appreciating a runner when he has just finished the race, rather than talking to him after 2 months is an example of this.

Let us see what happens if we do not show appreciation in time. Once, a manager approached his marketing person around 11 a.m. and said, "Well, my friend, you handle customers very well. I saw what you did the other day. A customer had come in. He was angry and volatile. But you pacified him within a few minutes and handled it well. Very good." This person just turns around and asks, **"Well, Sir, when was this?"** The boss thought he would motivate the employee by bringing up something good that he had done some time ago. But it backfired as the employee did not even remember when the incident took place. In the end, what the manager got was, "When was this?" This revert from the employee took the steam out of that motivational statement the boss intended to make.

Why did this happen? Because his boss did not show appreciation when the event happened or near to the event. Let us assume, at 11 a.m., the boss sees the employee doing some good work, and at around 11.30 a.m., he tells the employee – "You have dealt with the customer very nicely and placated him even though he was very angry and volatile. Keep up the good work! You are a role model for others." Now, the boss' motivational statement means a lot to the employee, and he would be ready to give VAS to his boss. **Immediate appreciation has substantial powers. The positive effect is lost when appreciation is delayed.**

We shall now see the importance of immediate reprimand.

Many times, when managers go on their walks around the plant, and they see someone not working as per the norms or making some mistakes, instead of bringing the error to the employee's notice, they do not say anything. However, they make a note of it in their diary. Then, probably after a month or so, when they notice the person making another mistake, they keep a record of it, and so on. At the time of appraisal, in April/May, they bring out the diary and say, "You have made so many mistakes; give me a reason why I should give you a good rating or a promotion?"

This approach is ineffective. The employee would say, "You should have told me this when I was making those mistakes. It would have helped me make changes in my performance. Now, after eight months, you are telling me when the damage has already been done." The boss would respond, "Yes. That's what I mean, that you're not doing a good job." The employee would retort, "Sir, you are the boss. You could have given me this feedback at that time. I would have changed my way of working, and this situation could have been avoided."

This is a common issue with some bosses. If there is a delay, even in reprimanding, then the effect is lost. So, immediate appreciation and immediate reprimand are two essential components of Extrinsic motivation. **Extrinsic motivation acts as a multiplying factor in personal effectiveness.** (Please refer to the formula for Personal Effectiveness given on page no. 29)

This also highlights the level of sensitivity we show to the people around us. So, how do we do it? For example - If any of my team members or any of my peer group members have done a good job, this should be acknowledged and spoken about at the earliest opportunity possible. Appreciation should be conveyed to that person, and such a gesture is also appreciated by team members, paving the way towards a healthy work climate.

An unwritten rule we must follow is to praise in public and reprimand in private.

In effect, immediate appreciation and immediate reprimand are highly recommended to obtain VAS from people around us.

References

- *https://corporatecommunicationexperts.com.au/importance-appreciation-workplace/*

- *https://www.achievers.com/blog/appreciation-in-the-workplace-why-it-matters/*

- *https://www.impactplus.com/blog/employee-appreciation-why-its-important-and-how-to-show-it*

- *https://hbr.org/2019/11/why-employees-need-both-recognition-and-appreciation*

2.4: Say What You Mean

Occasionally, we see some people thinking of triangles and talking in squares. When this is being done, many times, people can sense the manipulation hidden, and it does not enable VAS. It may ensure support initially, mainly because of the position or chair the person holds. However, this kind of support is short-lived.

It is essential to tell people why we are doing things and what the objective is, without using a façade. Very often, when we want to get work done from our subordinate(s), we say, "You know, the boss wants it," or "the boss has asked me to get this work done." The motive is to prompt the other person(s) to do the work quickly. The other person starts the task with full dedication. However, the second time they hear the same statement, they become wary and begin to sense the truth behind the 'boss' statement. By the third time, we have lost the power to get the work done. We have lost the power and respect of our position. Later, when we want some work done, the subordinate may ask, "Has the boss asked for it? Does he want it? Then I will do it." They will not comply with our requests. In terms of voluntary active support, it is necessary to be authentic in communication, which we have summarised in point no. 2.2 above, 'Be true to others.'

The first impression we make is, to be honest and upfront in all types of relationships in which we engage daily. This does not mean we should be blunt, rude, offensive or insensitive. When we don't say what we truly mean, we will experience less overall satisfaction with our environment. If my boss asks me whether I want coffee in the meeting, and if, out of courtesy, I say, "No, thanks." Later, I could sense tiredness in the meeting and wished I had said, "I would love some!" which would have been a better and truthful answer.

Another aspect is that we are often very cautious communicators when honesty truly is the best policy. When we mean what we say, it shows and allows us to gain more confidence in ourselves. It is better to speak from a place of honesty and then watch how our relationships and environments improve, day by day.

We live in a society where people prefer to be nice rather than truthful. But this niceness is not what will help the person improve. On the contrary, niceness will not help us avoid conflict. If I want VAS from people around me, I need to believe whatever I am saying - after all, I cannot get people to listen to me when I am pursuing a half-baked idea. "Say what you mean and mean what you say" is a trait of an effective communicator. It implies that we say things that we wholeheartedly believe in. This is a surefire way of getting VAS from people around us.

(Figure no.20: Say what you mean)

Occasionally, we put on a façade of listening and continue to insist on what the subordinate must do. The dialogue could look like this – "I have heard you in full, however, listen to what I am saying. You must complete the job in three days." What the subordinate was trying to say was that he had to go out of town for important personal work and would not be available for the next two days. This is manipulation of another kind, where seemingly, the boss has not heard a single word of what the subordinate was saying.

To gain VAS on a sustainable basis, we must communicate authentically and **say what we mean.**

References

- *https://www.elitedaily.com/life/say-mean-mean-say/813159*

- *https://themindfool.com/say-what-you-mean-and-mean-what-you-say/*

Getting Voluntary Active Support From People – Part III

3. MANAGING PERFORMANCE

3.1: "SWOT" Analysis of Self and Subordinates

In business, we often conduct a SWOT analysis. A SWOT analysis is a framework used to evaluate a company's competitive position and then develop a strategic plan to address these areas. SWOT stands for strengths, weaknesses, opportunities, and threats. One can apply the same process to one's team members, and this generates high VAS when strengths and weaknesses (areas for development) are communicated to them.

(Figure no.21: SWOT analysis of self and subordinates)

Another way to find strengths in people are the answers to the question of whether we have a proper placement of employees. Similarly, an added benefit while focusing on areas of development of team members would be, identifying if any of these members are better suited for another role. The manager can initiate this while having one-on-one meetings with employees, where job satisfaction could be discussed and constructive feedback provided on areas of improvement.

Additionally, it is possible to consider training activities such as on-the-job training, classroom training, and off-site training to further the skill levels of our employees. This is a spin-off because our real intention in this book has been to get VAS from people, which is ensured when we communicate their SWOT to them

Finally, while working on threats team members are facing individually, it is possible to proactively mitigate them. This, I consider an offshoot while the primary motive of getting VAS remains.

The third quadrant of the Johari Window is known as the blind quadrant, in a sense that I could be blind to my faults, and when somebody gives me feedback, I become aware of it. This is an important element in VAS, and I'm going to state how and why it is necessary to be sensitive to the strengths and weaknesses of self and others. We all know that strengths lead to opportunities and weaknesses lead to threats. Of course, it is a different matter that these days we don't say weaknesses; we call them areas of development or improvement. In giving feedback, we can use the 'sandwich' approach, which is one strength followed by an area of development.

When I hear about my strengths from others, it builds my morale. On the other hand, if I am made aware of my area of development, it helps me to grow. This fact, when leveraged, can give rise to a high degree of VAS. I often feel all line managers and HR managers must master this skill of giving and receiving feedback.

For example, if I had to give feedback to my subordinate, indicating that he or she is not a good team worker, then I would start with a compliment about the person. I would say, 'I find that you are a very good solo performer, and you complete all the projects on time. I am very happy with your work. However, I find that in cases where I have asked you to work with two or three other people, the results are far from satisfactory.

Another example of giving feedback to my subordinate following the same method would be as follows:

"Out of the ten meetings your group had planned, I find that you did not attend seven of them. The job was done, but your presence and contribution were not seen. I don't know whether you have been avoiding these meetings or you are not interested and find it difficult to work as a team. Let me tell you, in today's world, it is teamwork that plays a massive role. Gone are the days when one could work solo and achieve heights of glory. Now it is not so. It would be beneficial for you to think about this and build team working characteristics into your work style".

I have found that this kind of feedback normally gets accepted very fast, and a behavioural change is noticed.

In our daily interactions, our sensitivity to others must increase. I used to keep a passbook-type document for each of my subordinates which has a credit and debit side. The credit side contains all the positive behaviours he/she exhibits, while on the debit side, I record all the negative ones. In the monthly one on one meetings, I would tell them their plusses and minuses in a sandwich feedback manner. Using this methodology, I was fortunate to get a high degree of VAS from my subordinates.

The same thing can be employed when we are talking to somebody in the family or social sphere.

Reference

- *https://www.forbes.com/sites/scholleybubenik/2019/03/13/gaining-a-competitive-edge-by-conducting-a-swot-analysis-on-your-workforce/?sh=3d429d8c380d*

3.2: Awareness Of Short-term and Long-term Goals

A short-term goal is something that one wants to do in a short period, maybe in a year. A long-term goal is something one wants to do further in the future, 3 years, 5 years, or 7 years hence.

In terms of getting VAS, our focus will be on showing the consequences of the present work that people are engaged in to bring about a change in their current behaviour, which leads to higher quality and productivity. There are two examples in the foregoing part of this chapter. Let us begin with a story that goes like this! Three masons were working at a construction site. When the first mason was asked, "What are you doing?" He replied, "Well, I'm joining bricks by sand and mortar - can't you see – why do you ask?" The second person was asked the same question. "My friend, what are you doing?" He answered, "Well, I must earn a living. I work here. I get paid for it and I feed my family and myself." Then the third person was asked, "What are you doing? He responded, "Sir, I am building a hospital." Now, the third person's work, both in terms of quantity and quality would be far superior to that of the first two. This person is aware of the objective and the importance of his contribution to it. As we go forward with our normal day-to-day work, we must tell people what the short-term and long-term goals of whatever we are doing.

(Figure no.22: Awareness about short term and long-term goals)

I would like to share my personal experience here. In a company I worked for, I found that the workmen at the buffing stage were not giving their best output, with the result that their productivity and quality of work were low. I wanted to know the root cause, hence asked few of them what was happening there. In a very bored and uninterested tone, one of them said, "We come to the factory in the morning, we punch our card. Then we work and when it's time to leave, we go home. We are polishing whatever comes to us. That's what we are paid for. What's more to be done? I could see that they were not investing fully in whatever they were doing.

I made it a point to take them to the paint shop, to show them what happens when the buffing is not done properly. They saw the results of their work. When the surface is not smooth, the putty cannot be uniformly applied and therefore, the paint does not stick to the surface. When the product reaches the customers, in a short while, they find the paint peeling off. It leads to customer returns. I even showed them some of the fans that had been returned and were in the queue for getting repainted (which means more expenditure and reduced profits for the company). When they saw all this, they understood the importance of what they were doing, how important their work was, and also how crucial it was to do quality work to ensure the goodwill of the company was not compromised in any manner. They were convinced they had a role to play in the overall scheme of things. From then on, productivity and the quality of work drastically improved.

In the business world, it is often said, **"Sharing the company's vision means less supervision."** When we share our vision with our people, they get automatically engaged with the work they are doing. They know their contribution matters, so they will give their best. This is one of the most powerful ways of getting Voluntary Active Support from people.

Reference

- *https://careerwise.minnstate.edu/mymncareers/finish-school/long-short-goals. html*

3.3: Give Suggestions a Patient Listening

This is important because I have found that even though we often profess to listen to suggestions that are being given, we never take the pains of finding out whether they can be implemented or not. In case of suggestions not being implemented, the reason behind it must be communicated to person who gave it. If the logic for non-acceptance is given, then the person will understand and not hesitate to give more suggestions in future. If suggestions are not given by team members, it may result in a loss to the company, as a whole. Employees must always be made to feel valued and empowered.

(Figure no. 23: Give suggestions a patient listening)

Making Listening a Habit for VAS

Listening to employees ensures that the employee takes initiative, is engaged and brings forth his creative side. Additionally, this helps in the retention of employees.

Let us contrast this with the brainstorming methodology, where people freely give ideas and suggestions. Then, we sift through them and decide - which ideas will be considered for implementation in the short term, medium term, and long term and communicate it accordingly.

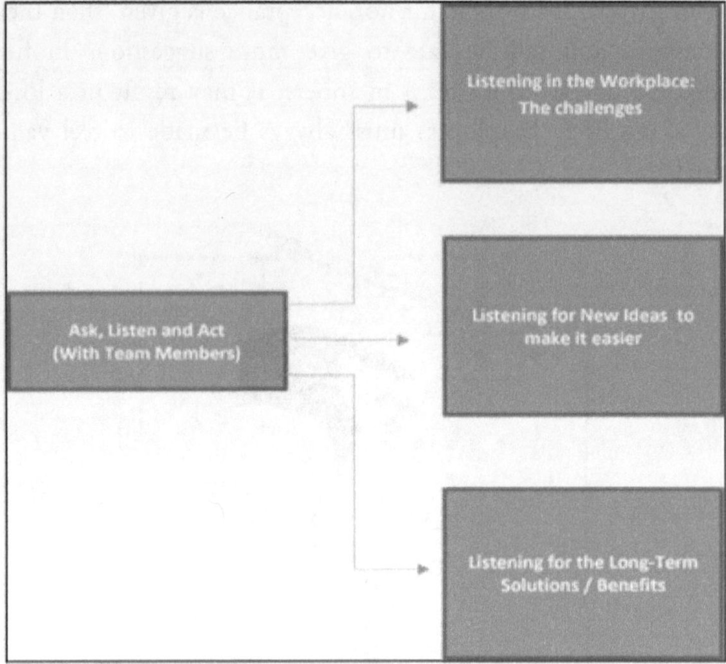

(Figure no.24: Listening – different perspectives.)

I once experimented with the brainstorming process. Owing to a decline in profits, the management asked us to cut costs. I decided that this had to be done with a certain amount of sensitivity.

There were 250 staff members. 10 sessions were conducted with 25 people in each group. From these sessions, we got about 1800 suggestions. Now this is a different process, where whatever people say is written down on the blackboard. A committee was then formed to sift through these suggestions and shortlist them into groups – short, medium, and long-term.

In such cases, it is not mandatory that every individual must be informed; however, the macro picture can be shared.

We can always learn from those around us, including our direct reports. Effective listening gives you knowledge and perspectives that increase leadership capacity. Listening to ideas from the workforce ensures three things in addition to getting VAS:

1. Shows we care about what they're saying and empathise with their feelings.

2. Creates a work environment of trust.

3. Makes employees more motivated and committed to their work.

The greatest advantage is, listening gives us knowledge and insights into the day-to-day reality of our employee's work life.

People freely give suggestions in an empowered environment. If one is sensitive enough, such ideas can surface during rounds on the shop floor, from meetings, group discussions, in the canteen, and almost anywhere. It makes sense to record suggestions given by employees and later find out their suitability for implementation.

Sometimes, suggestions may take a month or two to fruition. During this intervening period, it is a good practice to keep the person informed on the status. This is the human element.

Many managers' do not take this seriously. Suggestions from team members are considered important or otherwise depending on the 'label' we have given them. Consequently, importance is given to suggestions from 'the blue-eyed boys,' whereas employees who are 'backbenchers,' are sometimes ignored.

The truth is that ideas can come from anywhere, from anyone. Who is to say where the next grand idea is going to come from?? If a suggestion is given or an idea is shared, it is better to record it, work on it, and decide whether to take it forward. Keeping employees informed builds trust and integrity in the organisation.

I remember a case when a person had asked me, "Why can't the manual chuck on my lathe machine be replaced with the pneumatic chuck or a hydraulic chuck? Wouldn't that be much easier?" So much effort is being spent on tightening and zeroing the job on the machine.

I converted this suggestion to a low-cost automation project and implemented it. This led to a win-win - the worker could work with less effort and productivity also went up.

As a Methods Engineer, I got credit for this activity. However, I made it a point to recognise the workers in the annual meeting in front of the entire gathering.

Thus, suggestions when properly captured, analysed, and implemented go a long way in creating a climate of getting VAS from people.

References

- *https://www.etechgs.com/blog/ask-listen-team/*

- *https://blog.shrm.org/blog/5-reasons-why-you-should-listen-to-your-employees*

- *https://www.betterup.com/blog/the-importance-of-listening-as-a-leader-in-the-digital-era#:~:text=Really%20listening%20to%20someone%20shows,and%20committed%20to%20their%20work.*

- *https://www.jodymichael.com/blog/improve-leadership-skills-through-active-listening/*

3.4: Better Planning with People

It is necessary to involve the teams in the execution planning phase. The first step here is communication, so that everybody is on the same page, and everyone understands the overall vision and how the work they are doing fits into the overall strategy.

(Figure no.25: Better planning with people)

The second step is to get alignment within the department and cross-departmental understanding so that nothing falls between two stools. The last step is group facilitation so that each member participates in articulating their agreement or reservations.

In essence, all these steps help build consensus in the team for the way forward.

Very often, during meetings with senior management, we are asked to commit to what will be the production, the sales for the quarter or annual sales and so on. What will be the expected levels of machinery uptime and downtime, etc.? When we say something in the meeting, we must keep our word. For this, without a doubt, we require our team's support.

In the next possible interaction with the team, we will normally inform them of the commitment(s) we made and that we must start working towards achieving it. The first (informal) reaction we often hear from team members is, "You have committed, so please tell us what to do." This is a loaded question which means that the team is not going to put in any creative effort from their side and the amount of voluntary active support goes down. The ownership becomes more 'mine' and less 'theirs.'

In such cases, I would ask my team beforehand what kind of figures regarding production, sales, etc., they would like to achieve and how much they can stretch themselves.

Let us take production targets for example. I would ask them, 'Last month we made 200. What numbers can we commit to this month?' The answer would be, "We can approximately make anywhere between 210 and 220." Another person might say, "No, no, we can never make 220 because the 'x' part, e.g., an important spare part for the grinding machine, has not come yet, as it is still stuck in Customs. So how can we commit?" In this fashion, in the group meeting, bottlenecks surface. However, by dialogue and discussion, a consensual agreement could be reached that the maximum we can go up to is 220. Since this is a consensus decision, now the entire team has a stake in it.

A saying thus goes, 'It is better to under-commit and over-deliver.' Accordingly, I would inform the management that we can get 215 units manufactured this month and I will see if I can push my team to 220. I then came back and thanked my team. The job then gets done with fewer hassles, less heartburn, and less micromanaging, and I can garner voluntary active support from my team members.

Communicating beforehand and involving people in setting targets is very crucial to get the work done. Secondly, interactions with people to see what we can do and what we cannot do is equally important. In this process, it becomes more of a group commitment than an individual commitment. This process requires some skill and foresight, with a dose of proactivity, and thus 'better planning with people' becomes a strong tool to get voluntary active support from people around us.

To get VAS from individuals and the team, we must define realistic engagement goals in everyday terms. It is a skill to weave engagement into daily interactions and activities by discussing how one wants employees to involve themselves with team tasks and goals at weekly meetings, planning sessions, and in one-on-ones.

References

- *https://www.liquidplanner.com/blog/7-ways-to-get-your-team-members-more-engaged/*

- *https://www.rhythmsystems.com/blog/annual-planning-9-tips-to-focus-align-your-team-with-a-great-plan*

<table><tr><td>

Chapter

9

</td><td>

Getting Voluntary Active Support from People – Part IV

</td></tr></table>

4. MANAGING CULTURE

4.1: Develop Lateral Understanding Among Peers

In my tenure with Crompton Greaves as well as Mahindra & Mahindra Ltd., I conducted two experiments in this area. I named it the Teaching Learning Community (TLC). How does it work? For example, in the maintenance department, we form a team of engineers, each one of them an expert in their field. One of the engineers chosen is very good at hydraulics, another at electrical engineering, the third at CNC machining, and so on.

(Figure no.26: Develop lateral understanding among peers)

These people come together voluntarily once a month for one hour. During that time, one person takes the stage and talks about his area of expertise to others for about 30 to 40 minutes, and 20 minutes are kept for questions and answers. Through 12 meetings, the net result of this exercise was; I found a quantum jump in the level of learning in this group. In the process, they learn something new, something of importance which will enable members to get a better understanding of how things work across verticals and how it can impact their work.

We very well know that information is power and when a person, say, an electrical engineer, understands the nuances of hydraulics, he tends to have an enhanced grip on his job. Added to this, each member of the group knows where the expertise lies and whom to approach in times of complicated breakdowns.

Teaching Learning Communities were formed in this manner at the engineering level. The second one I formed with commercial personnel. The third one was at the Corporate Level, where people from the Secretarial, Taxation, Treasury, and CFO's office, all got together, and one of them would share their expertise in that half-hour to 40 minutes as detailed earlier with Q/A for 20 minutes. A window of broader knowledge was thus made available to every single staff working in the corporate office, and I have seen people enjoying the sessions as well as increasing their knowledge base, which they know would stand them in good stead later in life.

It is one of the best ways of organisational learning, where the team learns, the individual learns, and the company experiences a quantum jump in the wisdom of its workforce. The other advantage is that, when people leave the company, their expertise, wisdom, and experience do not go with them. It remains with the people they have worked with and associated themselves with.

The flip side of what can go wrong here is maintaining the enthusiasm of people. Once they have finished round one, what do we do next? Does it stop here? My suggestion would be to ask members from other TLCs to come and talk as guest faculty. The sessions don't stop after one group is done; they move from group to group, where people share their subject knowledge and answer queries.

Another great advantage the company gets is that people move towards platform speaking, which many of us are not very comfortable with. They become more confident in sharing views and speaking in front of an audience. When such sessions come up, half an hour of speaking about their topic becomes mandatory. When their turn comes, they must volunteer to speak. Such sessions are a great way to enhance or sharpen their communication and presentation skills at the same time.

An added advantage is that if one must speak for one hour, then he/she must prepare in advance. The preparation involves going in-depth into the subject matter and being up to date about the latest changes or additions that may have come about. This research would help him/her become much more experienced in his/her subject and much more knowledgeable in that area. After preparation, he/she would be able to cascade that knowledge and experience to others.

The underlying principle of a Teaching Learning Community is that we develop a lateral understanding of different subjects among our peer group.

Since we are now aware and have gained insights from the various TLC sessions we have attended, we have started understanding the nuances and know where the shoe is pinching if or when we face issues in our work area. Apart from this, when we move on to senior positions, for example, if somebody becomes a maintenance manager, he is going to handle electrical, mechanical, and civil, all together. He can do this easily to an extent because by this time he has already learned from the others. Thus, he can manage his new role very well. This is another advantage of having TLCs. All these come under the method of developing lateral understanding among Peer Groups, which is a fantastic way of getting voluntary active support from people around us.

Another version of TLCs is described by some authors (See references) as "Peer Learning." Peer learning can be formal or informal, but it always involves some sort of collaboration between two or more peers. It is a great way to boost employee engagement and collaboration while also encouraging learning and development. Plus, it helps create an environment of trust between employees, which is essential for any successful business.

This type of collaboration has been proven in certain areas to be more effective than traditional learning methods, as it allows learners to gain different perspectives on a subject matter and exchange and build upon each other's ideas while staying focused on the task at hand. The benefits of peer learning go beyond just collaboration and respect, though. It also helps employees become better problem solvers by teaching them how to work together and think critically about their ideas. It encourages creativity, which can lead to innovation in the workplace.

In summary, TLCs that embody peer learning can become a great with can provide substantial contribution to Voluntary Active Support (VAS).

Knowledge sharing is the transfer of tacit knowledge between employees, and hence, employees will develop considerable knowledge as they grow in their roles. Peer-to-peer learning encourages knowledge sharing, and so critical know-how is retained within organisations even when employees leave. This is the biggest advantage companies can reap.

Additionally, we get:

- Peer-to-peer learning, an affordable option that requires less money than hiring instructors for workshops and training sessions.

- High-potential employees will validate their knowledge by sharing it with others.

- There is also a possibility that high-potential employees can become top trainers within the company.

- Strong peer relationships within the company, which helps increase loyalty and retention.

Reference

- https://www.togetherplatform.com/blog/peer-learning-benefits

4.2: This is not My Job' & 'I Don't Know' Syndromes

Often, we hear at the workplace the sentence, "It's not my job." This approach may help one to avoid extra work; however, it subtly prevents one from advancing in his/her career since the label comes across as someone unwilling to go the extra mile.

One can grant the possibility that there is too much to do, and therefore it does not make sense to take up more work and at the same time deliver quality. In such cases, it is recommended that we point to another colleague who can help the employee who has come for support.

The fundamental issue is to avoid saying, "It's not my job" (in effect - not my responsibility), as it automatically sends a negative message. Refraining from using the term - 'that's not my job' could lead to multiple benefits for self and organisation. The best way to overcome this syndrome is to develop a sense of accountability for any task assigned.

From a manager's perspective, it is a big challenge to tactfully engage employees and get voluntary active support for additional tasks.

(Figure 27: 'This is not my job' & 'I don't know' syndromes)

The expectation is that the employee understands the need, clarifies doubts regarding the task at hand, collaborates and communicates with positive intent, owns the issue, organises the work, and while doing so, understands others' viewpoints and acts responsibly. (Thus the 'victim mentality' is left behind.)

When I say, "This is not my job," indirectly I mean that I am not willing to take responsibility. Another way to respond would be – 'Well, this does not come under my portfolio now. However, what I can do is, I will take you to the person who can address your need.' The person who has approached me feels happy and would be willing to give me voluntary active support when I require it. This I have experienced several times.

All of us want active support, not passive support. When somebody asks me for some help or support, I will not say, "I don't know." I would rather say, "I will find out" or "I will support you when I get more clarity on the subject." 'I don't know' sounds very negative and in no way ensures any kind of support.

From my experience, two more concepts can generate voluntary active support from people. One of them is following the dictum, **'laugh with people, not at people.'** The other one is, **'to avoid gossip at all costs',** and the way we define gossip here is – talking about someone who is not present in the discussion.

In summation, all the above four ways of managing culture, generates substantial Voluntary Active Support, because the trust levels rise exponentially.

References

- *https://www.linkedin.com/pulse/overcome-its-my-job-syndrome-mansi-m*

- *https://www.themuse.com/advice/heres-a-better-and-less-whiny-way-to-say-thats-not-my-job*

- *https://www.plantservices.com/articles/2019/how-to-change-the-thats-not-my-job mindset/#:~:text=There%20are%20a%20few%20ways,to%20act%20and%20 ask%20questions*

4.3: Making People Aware of Costs

I know of a major public sector manufacturing organisation in the south of India, where labels were affixed to machines, indicating their price. For example, "This machine costs rupees one crore, 50 lakhs, 30 lakhs," and so forth. The rationale behind this practice is a hypothesis suggesting that when machine operators observe these labels, they become aware of the costly asset they are handling. As a result, they are more likely to adhere to the standard operating procedures, leading to reduced rejections and increased productivity and they are motivated to maintain a high standard of cleanliness on and around the machines.

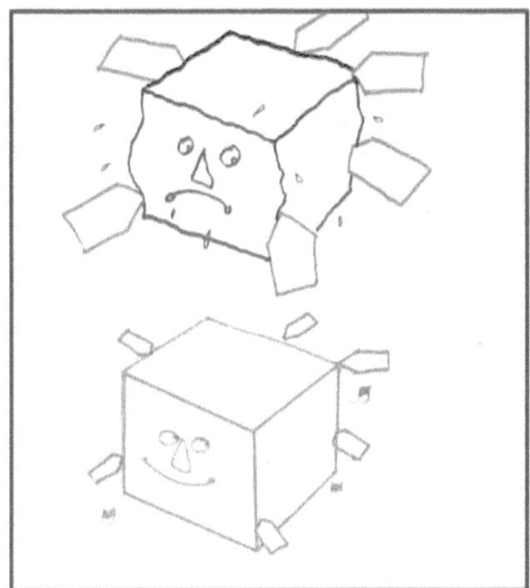

(Figure 28: Making people aware of costs)

Let me narrate an interesting experiment which inadvertently led me on a journey towards achieving zero defects.

The entire episode unfolded as follows:

In the paint shop, I queried one of the painters:

Me: "How many rejections do you typically encounter during a full shift?"

Painter: "Around 3 to 4%."

Me: "What does 3 to 4% translate to?"

Painter: "With an output of 200, it means six to eight blades are rejected."

Me: "What happens to these rejected blades?"

Painter: "They undergo repainting."

Me: "Are you aware of the cost of repainting?"

Painter: "No, nobody has informed me."

Me: "Listen, for each blade, we incur an additional cost of eight rupees to rectify it. How much do you earn daily?"

Painter: "50 rupees."

Me: "So, if six blades from your lot are rejected, that amounts to 48 rupees. Essentially, the company is paying you 50 rupees while incurring a loss of 48 rupees. Do you comprehend?"

This revelation startled the painter. He had never been enlightened on this matter before, nor had he contemplated it. Once made aware, he began pondering the situation.

Leaving him to his thoughts, I revisited the topic after a few days and inquired, "Do you have a plan to reduce rejections?" He affirmed, proposing his first idea - maintaining a constant pressure during the painting process. He noted that there was a slight pressure drop each time he pressed the trigger when using pressure-assisted guns (a normal occurrence).

Recognising this as a valid concern, I procured a new pressure gauge and fixed the pressure at 60 psi. The painter expressed satisfaction, believing this adjustment would help minimise rejections. My initial success came after 14 days when rejections decreased from 6% to 4%. (Please note, it was a misconception on the part of the painter that variations in air pressure were causing paint defects. Fluctuations in pressure are typical when the trigger is pressed.)

On further prodding the painter for further reduction in rejections, he said, "the raw paint can, which comes to me for use on the components, is not perhaps tested because I cannot see any seal or stamp of quality on every 20-litre can I get. An entire batch of 200 litres is tested and then given for us to use". To give heed to this painter, I organised a few cans with the quality stamped on them and asked him to proceed. The result was miraculous – rejections dropped from 4% to 2%. The journey from two to zero is very interesting.

To my question, why can't we go to zero? The painter had three postulates:

1. What will I stand to gain?

   My answer – pride in the work.

2. If I give zero once, I will be made to give zero every day, every shift, and that I cannot sustain.

   My response – I called a local union leader and the supervisor and told them that this was an experiment that we were doing, and the painter should not be pressured to give zero every time.

3. I am a human being - one or two mistakes in a hundred are natural.

My response – when you go to a dentist to get one bad tooth removed, the experienced dentist, by mistake, pulls out the wrong tooth. Now tell me, will you forgive him because he is a human being? The painter said, 'No way' and that was a breakpoint. He started thinking about zero defects, and as my luck would have it, he achieved zero defect one week after this episode. I felt overjoyed, and my hypothesis was validated, namely, **that zero defect lies in the mind of the person.**

The same experiment was repeated in the packing shop, where I had seen packing material and other things scattered and lying hither and thither. I just picked up one or two of them and asked them what the cost of this material would be when we buy it from the packing supplier. They were not able to get the cost. I showed them the purchase order. This piece costs Rs.2/- per piece, and Rs.2/- is now lying on the floor. Who is responsible for this? Why is it that we are not aware of how much money is going down the drain due to our negligence? **If this was your company, would you do this?**

In one of our meetings, a very senior person in quality control brought up this topic. He said, "You know we are having 4% rejections." I asked, "What is the monetary value of these rejections?" He was quiet for some time. I said, "Please work out the number. What is the meaning of this 4%?" The cost of the 4% rejections amounted to a whopping 6 lakhs of rupees.

My conversation with him went thus:

Me: If this was your company, would you allow this to happen? What are your plans to mitigate rejections? (The purpose of asking this question was to reduce rejections and achieve zero defects.)

He: It is very difficult. Let me see what I can do. We made some changes last year. From 4%, the rejections came down to 3.8%.

Me: These micro-reduction in rejection levels have no meaning. If this were your company, would you be satisfied with these figures? Or would you aim for 1% or 1.5% from the outset? Consider yourself a CEO and tell me whether you would be able to tolerate the wastage.

Thus, I came to the conclusion that, people give their best when they become aware of the costs involved.

In meetings, I have often heard managers say, 'In this meeting, there are ten of us. If we add the hourly salary of all of us together, that will be 2.4 lakhs. So, every hour we spend in the meeting here is going to consume 2.4 lakhs of company money.' So true! It is observed, sometimes, when officers and managers are discussing strategies and solutions, the meetings go on and on without adding value. Occasionally, major time is spent in discussing trivial matters. Are all meetings productive, and do they justify the ROI (Return on Investment)?

Thus, we see that "Make people aware of costs" can work nicely for generating VAS when we instil a cost-conscious mindset and behaviours in employees throughout the organisation.

The workforce may have effective cost-cutting ideas but bringing them to the surface requires considerable employee communication and engagement skills. In explaining why cost-cutting is necessary, we need to translate the business case for cost-cutting into terms that are meaningful for all employees.

Reference

- https://www.bcg.com/publications/2021/sustaining-cost-conscious-culture

4.4: Disseminating Product Information

Learning about product knowledge can help internal employees increase their level of engagement. Additionally, when employees have a solid understanding of each product, it's easier for them to suggest improvements to the product or its packaging.

Here are some important points for employees to know about company products:

   a. Pricing structure

   b. Models, styles, and colours available

   c. Product uses

   d. Service, warranty, and repair information

(Figure 29: Disseminating Product Information)

Drawing from my experience, I have found that disseminating information about the product can garner voluntary active support in a significant way. A couple of experiments I conducted on this topic, way back in 1987-88. The theme considered was - How do we increase the sense of belongingness of people to the organisation? The first experiment was on sharing product knowledge – What happens when we give the right product knowledge to our employees, not just peripheral but in-depth knowledge. Can this arouse their curiosity?

I conducted a few sessions for the supervisors, wherein I asked – "Do you know about the ceiling fan that we are making?"

They said, "Yes, yes, we do. We have been working here for so many years. We know what a fan is." Great! Then I asked, "When the regulator is on 1 (lowest speed) and when the regulator is on 6 (full speed), in which position does the fan draw more current, and therefore in which position are we going to pay a higher energy bill?"

I received a few answers like, if the regulator position is on 2 or 3, that means there is resistance, and some voltage drop occurs in overcoming the resistance. Therefore, the current consumed will be higher at the lowest speed. **A little reflection will tell us that the reverse is true.** This means that when there is no resistance, the fan runs at full speed and here the maximum current is drawn. This becomes a revelation as there is a new learning here.

Another question was put forward to a team working in a fan manufacturing company; Supposing your neighbour calls you and tells you;

"Look at my fan – it is rotating anti-clockwise." He knows you are from the fan industry and have been working in a fan manufacturing company as a supervisor for many years. "Can you solve this problem?" There were not many answers. Only silence followed. One person, after great coaxing, said, "Hey, we should change the condenser leads and it will solve the problem." He was correct, but this came only from one person in the group of 20 or 25 supervisors! It also leaves room for others to introspect on their lack of knowledge, despite many years in the field.

Here, I found the employees' thirst to know more about the product and company substantially increased. I then brought the marketing information to them including strong markets and not-so-strong markets, pricing, advertising, and the kind of contribution that each of our products are making. I continued about how money is converted to goods and how we convert goods back to money, thereby completing a full cycle.

I have found that when employees get product and marketing knowledge and relevant sections of manufacturing, they become more engaged in their work and the efficiency, productivity, and quality go up. VAS happens and as a result of the above, it is a complete win-win, mainly with the workforce and the union.

It is good to evaluate employees' product knowledge at regular intervals. Thorough knowledge of the company's products allows employees to connect their role to the ultimate product which goes to the customer. It also allows the employees, particularly on the manufacturing side, to give creative inputs to product designers. It will be pertinent to mention here that when employees fully understand a product and its market, they advocate the company's products in their social networks with gusto.

References

- *https://www.indeed.com/career-advice/career-development/products-knowledge*

- *https://whatfix.com/blog/product-knowledge-training/*

Chapter 10

The Bonus Chapters Start Now!

Bonus Chapters: Getting Voluntary Active Support from bosses and peers.

We have just seen 9+7 = 16 ways of getting Voluntary Active Support (VAS). If we look at the wheel below, the methods described so far apply to all the areas of the wheel.

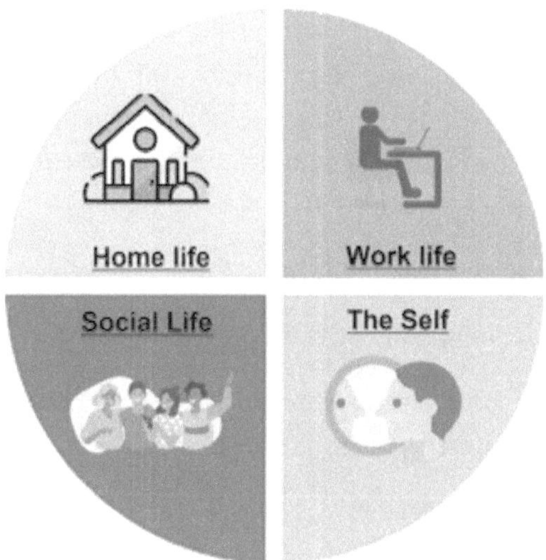

(Figure 30: Four domains of life)

However, in work-life, we meet and interact with three kinds of people:

a. The bosses or boss-level executives.

b. Peers.

c. Subordinates.

We may require specialised methods to get VAS from the above categories. Needless to add, in the social domain, we have 1) neighbours; 2) relatives &

3) friends. In this book, we have not dealt with the social domain in great depth – suffice to say that the 9+7 = 16 ways would be very much applicable in every domain.

We are now going to focus on (in the above order) bosses, as they form a major part of our working day, at least in our minds, and very often, they are present as unseen guests at the dining table or in the drawing room. Some surefire ways of managing bosses have been described in the next chapter. For peers, in the experience of the author, the 9+7 = 16 ways are sufficient and sustaining. We would welcome views on the experiences readers share to take this hypothesis further. After bosses, we would be dealing with some techniques for getting VAS from subordinates. So, fasten your seatbelt and let's zoom ahead.

Failure to manage the boss often results to misunderstandings, wastage of time and effort, inability to convert one's ideas into action, lack of promotion, and reduced influence within and outside the organisation. Common reasons include a lack of clarity on common goals and objectives due to inadequate communication between them, resulting in misunderstanding of expectations and roles.

There are some typical ways of managing the boss, which include:

a. Knowing the boss's way of working, behaviour, and communication.

b. One should be aware of what is expected of oneself and what one would expect if he/she is in the boss's position.

c. Know the boss's priorities.

d. Effective communication with the boss: Know the preferred way to receive information. Some prefer to read, and others listen. If the boss prefers reading, write an e-mail or a formal letter as the situation demands. If the boss prefers to listen, a brief chat is called for. In both cases, substantiating with evidence, (facts and figures), becomes helpful.

e. Keep the boss briefed on one's activities and major events so that there are no surprises.

f. Request feedback on the activities currently in process. Providing feedback to seniors is a difficult task. As one moves up, honest feedback becomes generally rare; hence, it will help the boss if one can provide honest feedback. **Please note: It is important to avoid unsolicited feedback.**

g. Dealing with disagreements professionally: Treating people with respect, even those with whom you disagree, gets respect and trustworthiness in return.

h. Collaborate: Meet regularly with one's boss and develop a professional relationship based on mutual trust and respect.

i. Initiative: Search for opportunities to contribute to problem-solving and innovation within the team/organisation. Remember, paradigm shifts are often made by individuals who are not directly involved with the problem or necessarily have subject expertise.

j. Being a player for all seasons and demonstrating positive behaviours especially during hard times, is useful.

k. Building trust is a tool of high priority that serves one in good times as well as in challenging times. It's not what we do when the boss is not looking that builds reputation, it's how and what we do when he's not looking that builds our character.

Acknowledgement: The authors of this article (Managing Bosses and Peers, namely Sanjiv Kumar, Vivek S. Adhish and Abhimanyu Chauhan) from where the foregoing notes have been taken, have thankfully acknowledged the usefulness of the book *HBR Guide to Managing Up and Across*. HBR Press. Boston 2013, in their work.

Among some of the tried and tested ways of getting VAS from bosses, the first is **Managing their Ego**. This is not as simple as it seems.

I will narrate an experience here – whenever I am not in agreement with my boss, and there are very strong reservations, rather than raising it in the meeting and creating a kind of argument, I would always ask for more time. I would say, "Boss, I have some reservations about whatever is being discussed – Let me put my thoughts together before I speak to you." This gives me the time to build consensus with few of my peers before I take it to the boss. This might not be possible every time. Sometimes, I was pressurised to immediately put across my point. In which case, I just give a small hint. Later in the evening, I would go to the boss with more details, more preparation, and whatever I wanted to say. I would avoid any confrontation at the meeting. Here, I ensure that the boss's ego is not hurt by contradicting him in a group situation. Occasionally, we get straight into an argument with the boss, and often, irrespective of the topic being discussed, the ego is hurt, and this would hamper getting VAS from bosses.

The second one is all about **managing the insecurity of bosses.** Each one of us, at times, is insecure, from the point of view of not achieving expected outcomes. These thoughts seem to be at the top of bosses' minds - "What will happen if ----?," How do I navigate this situation? And so on.

The subordinate must manage this insecurity. A classic example I will give here: Once, when I was doing the second shift, a small fire broke out in the plant. This news had to be conveyed to the General Manager, and everyone was worried about how he would react. That was the time I realised one can talk in a way that does not increase the bosses' insecurity.

So, instead of saying, Sir. Sorry for waking you up at this time of the night - a fire has broken out on the premises. This would let off a trigger and could make my boss jump out of his bed, saying, "What happened? Was there any loss?" etc., etc.

Instead, I said, "This is just for your information. There was a small fire in the premises which has already been controlled. We called the fire brigade. However, it was sent back since we could use our resources to put out the fire promptly. All who were present came forward and supported us. However, there has been a minor damage to the paint booth, and this will be investigated. The lost production will be made up by working extra shifts on the other two paint booths.

I wondered how such an act of mine was possible at the beginning of my career as a trainee. Now, in hindsight, I realise that I applied the knowledge gained from a recent fire drill and ensured that the situation was brought under control. After containing the damage, I went on the phone (we only had landlines then, no cell phones) to report the incident to my boss.

This kind of 'controlled conversation' gave confidence to my boss that things were being handled properly. At the same time, his insecurity was managed. There have been several occasions since then where I had to use prudence, ensuring that I didn't make the person further insecure about results. It does not mean that we paint a rosy picture. However, we need to put things forward in a manner that the 'secure' feeling of the boss remains unhindered.

The third one is a bit off track. Here, I am saying that we need to **manage the idiosyncrasies** of bosses. People behave in a certain manner, which sometimes appears out of place. For example – micro-managing to the extreme or demanding long reports every week, following up at 8 am for what was discussed the previous night at 9 pm. Sounds idiotic. The answer lies in having coping strategies.

I have had bosses who were very bullish micro-managers. Every time they passed by my table they would like to know what the status is. This became very irritating. There is a metaphor which says – It is easier to ride the horse in the direction it is going and make a big U-turn rather than turning abruptly. The secret is (I have experienced this) to go with the flow, build rapport with the boss, and convince him that his goals are my goals and that I would spare no effort in supporting him and my peers in achieving departmental targets.

I have also come across managers who say don't give me a call unless something is super important. If you call me, I will assume something is wrong. I almost got trapped in a catch-22 situation when I did not inform my boss of a problem on the shop floor, and this boomeranged heavily. When he came to know about it, he reprimanded me strongly. I realised this balancing act on a tightrope, hence made up a strategy to inform only critical incidences and that too, without delay.

Every boss has his own style of functioning, and one must adapt to these individual styles. This enables us to work well with them and, in a way, get voluntary active support from them. We have seen three right now - managing insecurities, managing idiosyncrasies, and managing ego. These three are primary. There are four more secondary ones, and I will be dealing with them in the ensuing pages.

1. We can also foster excellent relationships with superiors if we follow some disciplines at the workplace. The first one is that occasionally, one should check the direction in which we are going, which means whether the KRAs and KPIs are aligned with the boss's goal sheet.

2. Another discipline is being more proactive, which means doing a job before it is even asked for. This shows that one can think ahead and align his/her perspective to the current needs of the organisation and take steps to execute them without being micro-managed. This really can build a good rapport with the boss.

3. Another hack (which I have found in my experience) - one should never surprise the boss, especially with any adverse news, even if it means information about a missed deadline or unfavourable events happening in the environment, which could affect the boss, especially when he is in an important meeting. It is always better to tell him before the meeting. It is always better to keep the boss in the loop as, if he comes to know about it from others, he/she will be very much annoyed.

4. I found this helpful - that one can go to the boss with solutions for problems at hand in terms of alternatives 'A', 'B', and 'C'. The boss may either select one of these or give his perspective as alternative 'D'. At the same time, he realises that I have done my homework in an attempt to solve the problem. This takes the boss-subordinate relationship to the next level.

5. Finally, we need to understand that it is mostly a rollercoaster ride for each one of us in the organisation. This includes our bosses, too. They, too, have their own challenges and stressful times to deal with. This awareness can lead to appropriate tactics in handling interpersonal relationships with the boss.

Al Coleman, Jr., author of Secrets to Success: The Definitive Career Development Guide for New and First-Generation Professionals, and Anita Attridge, a Five O'clock Club career and executive coach, shared tips for impressing your boss and winning his or her approval.

Coleman says: **"Consistently demonstrate an interest in the success of your boss and the organisation you work for."**

References

- *https://www.ncbi.nlm.nih.gov/pmc/articles/PMC4317975/*

- *https://roubler.com/resources/blog/managing-boss-peers/*

Chapter 11

Managing Subordinates

Getting VAS from Subordinates entails three essentials.

1. **Managing the dichotomy between concern for task and concern for people.**

   The Blake & Mouton Grid plots a manager's or leader's degree of task-centredness versus their person-centredness and identifies five different combinations of the two and the leadership styles they produce. It is also known as the Managerial Grid or Leadership Grid and was developed in the early 1960s by management theorists Robert Blake and Jane Mouton as illustrated in the diagram below:

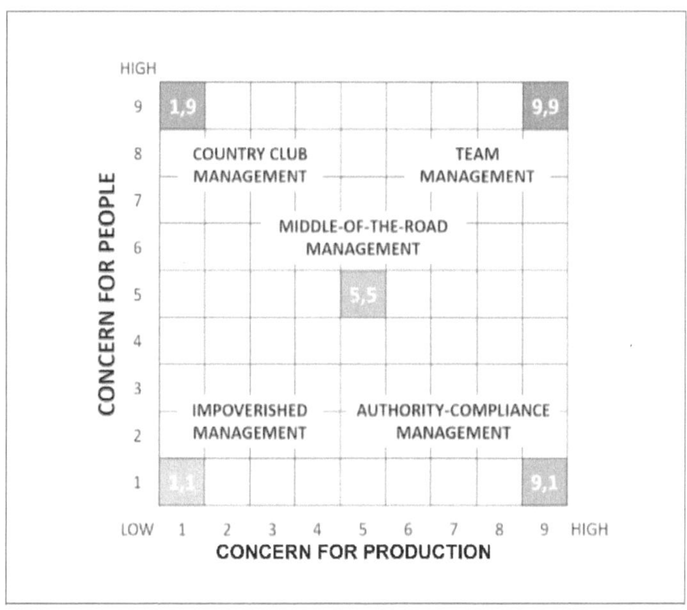

(Figure 31: The Blake Mouton Grid)

(Source & Reference: https://www.business-to-you.com/blake-mouton-managerial-grid/)

The model is based on two behavioural dimensions:

Concern for People: this is the degree to which a leader considers team members' needs, interests, and areas of personal development when deciding how best to accomplish a task.

Concern for Task: this is the degree to which a leader emphasises concrete objectives, organisational efficiency, and high productivity when deciding how best to accomplish a task.

When people are committed to, and have a stake in, the organisation's success, their needs and production needs coincide. This creates an environment based on trust and respect, which leads to high satisfaction, motivation, and excellent results.

The 9/9 boss, in the managerial grid, can balance both the pulls, equally well, which is, concern for task and concern for people. This is one element that a person must learn to manage subordinates very well.

Let's take an example - when a subordinate asks to go early and he/she must finish several tasks before leaving. We can look for a win-win situation by working together with a third colleague and/or ensuring that the job is done in the person's absence. Another option - give instructions to finish the job from home.

2. **Need for flexibility and control at the same time.**

Flexibility can give rise to creative and productive ideas, whereas control produces predictable results and execution in a possibly well-defined manner. However, we need to have a balance between flexibility and control in managing subordinates. Too much control can lead to micromanagement, and this may hurt the relationship between boss and subordinate. Whereas too much flexibility can prove to be an obstacle to reaching company objectives.

3. **Giving constructive feedback as early as possible**

Path-breaking work has been done by two scientists (psychologists Joseph Luft, (1916–2014) and Harrington Ingham, (1916–1995), who created the Johari Window in 1955.

We will be focusing on quadrant number 3, which is the blind quadrant, in the sense that one could be blind to one's faults. Awareness dawns when somebody gives feedback, to that effect.

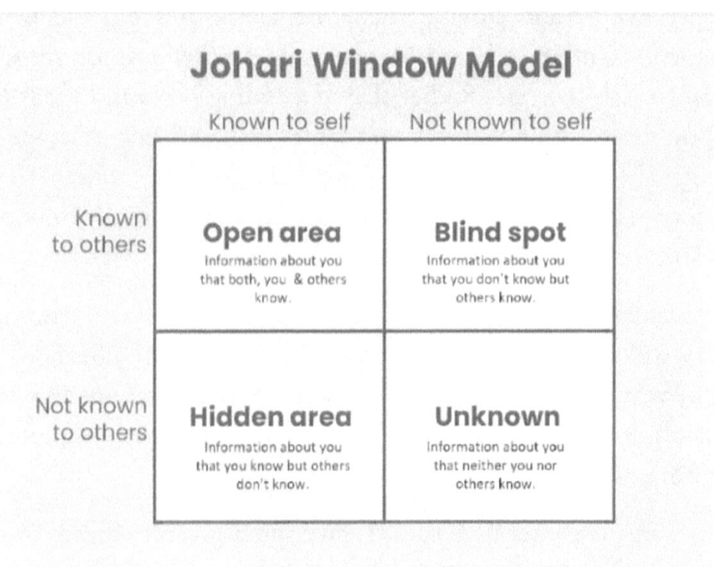

(Figure 32: Johari Window – Giving Constructive Feedback)
(Source & Reference: https://fundakoca.medium.com/johari-window-9f874884fc10)

For giving feedback, we can follow three simple rules.

1. Start with a positive feedback and then proceed to the areas of improvement.

2. Give examples of both plus and minus to the subordinate.

   (Points no. 1 & 2 have been explained in detail in section 3.1, 'SWOT' analysis of self and subordinates)

3. Give feedback as close to the event as possible.

We need not wait for the yearly or biannual appraisal to take place. In my experience, I have found that it is better to keep a diary of the debits and credits of each person working in the department. I capture the pluses on one side and the minuses on the other, just like a bank passbook. These points are then communicated to the employee using a typical sandwich approach. It means that we must become more sensitive to the people around us. As managers, we must notice people doing the right things as well as observe areas of improvement and give feedback appropriately.

The very aspect of noticing people doing the right things enhances the trust between boss and subordinate. One needs to avoid the temptation of saying, for example,' **I heard from so and so** that you are spending too much time in the canteen'. Rather than depending on hearsay, it is better to take responsibility and say, 'I saw you (and genuinely, one must see that) in the canteen sitting there for a long time. I do not know whether you were waiting for a client. What if this is happening more often for my comfort? What is your response to this and what is your plan'?

This will encourage the subordinate to come up with an action plan, or at least he will say that I will stop doing it, which is the ultimate objective of the interaction anyway. Having constructive conversations like this with subordinates enhances the quality of the boss-subordinate relationship and fosters VAS.

Now, when it comes to bosses, I have often given feedback to my boss whenever he asked me the question, "What do you think about my way of working"? It was very humble of my boss to ask for this feedback, but that was his way of improving himself. These meetings were held at least once in six months. In one of the meetings, I told him, "Sir, you are quite proficient in your domain of work management. However, what I don't appreciate is that people around don't see any value in it when you shout at people in the presence of their peers and subordinates. This is very hurtful. I, too, have faced this and find it very difficult to digest that I get a firing from you in front of my own subordinates and peers. It not only lessens my credibility in their eyes, but it also makes it difficult to get work done from them later. I don't know whether something can be done about this, but if something could be done, it would be beneficial for all involved." This feedback was given directly to him, and it appealed to him. It prodded him to change his style of functioning. The third quadrant of the Johari Window thus becomes very 'live' in our daily situations.

Bosses don't automatically gain respect from their employees; they need to earn respect by demonstrating that they value employees and prioritise their growth. Managers can earn more respect by improving their communication with employees and explaining strategic decisions as deemed fit.

Some of the known methods in addition to the above, are as follows:

a. Be consistent in the style of managing people for predictability

b. Being fair and firm

c. Admitting mistakes – shows the bosses' vulnerability

d. Recognising small wins

e. Seeking out feedback and acting on them visibly

f. Delegate by results expected – no micromanaging

g. Percolating praise received down the line, however, making the blame buck stop at one's table

References

- *https://www.freshbooks.com/hub/leadership/gain-respect-from-employees*

- *https://www.mindtools.com/pages/article/newLDR_73.htm*

Chapter 12

Creating A VAS Culture – Some Groundwork

1. Looking at inter-departmental harmony

2. Sowing the seeds of an SMT way of working

3. A culture that promotes teamwork

1. Looking at Inter-departmental Harmony

Inter Team Collaboration – It is often assumed that departments work closely together, e.g., Production and Marketing. However, often, they seem to be at loggerheads. The same situation can happen between Production and Materials, Production and Maintenance, and even Design and Marketing!

A method called confrontation meetings can be adopted to prevent dysfunctional behaviour.

In a typical session, two warring groups with their middle management personnel are seated next to each other. The bosses of the respective departments take seats at the back. They just observe what is happening, and they come in and speak only at the end.

Continuing, from my experience, I first invite any one person from the first group to say something positive about the other group. For example, the person says, "Yes, marketing is vital to the company, and they bring in the money." I ask for another plus point, and they say, "They are doing a good job despite problems in product, quality, and delivery. That is something we appreciate".

I then ask the marketing team to say something positive about production. They may say, "They listen to us, and we get the supplies whenever we want. There are few delays; however, overall, they are quite passionate about their work."

The next part of the process is to go for the negatives. I ask someone from the production team what is not working. They start by saying, "Well, there are issues - marketing does not give us the required time for delivery. First, they ask for red pieces, and then suddenly, they change it to black. Now, the fact is that a batch of red is being produced in the paint plant, and for us to change the colour to black, it takes at least ten days to restart. Such a quick changeover is not possible. Therefore, we are requesting sufficient lead time to change over batches.

Then I shift my focus to the marketing team and ask; what is going wrong with production? They say that, well, production people are very rigid; they are not flexible. Customer requirements are very dynamic, and they do not resonate with the same agility. We are here to cater to customers' needs. When prodded for more details, the marketing team says, "Whenever we give them something, they will not even revert to us whether the job can be done or not. They normally keep quiet, and when the time comes for delivery, they say it cannot be done. Because of their laid-back attitude, we lose valuable time, and, in the process, we lose the customer too. This is unhealthy.

In aggregate terms, this conversation about the positives and negatives of each department is initiated, and both points of view are recorded.

Feedback for every point or situation raised is sought in a facilitative manner. I proceed to the finer aspects of resolutions, e.g., what is the lead time that satisfies both the groups - say three weeks? This will be recorded on the board for later follow-up. This process continues to a point wherein there are no unresolved negative instances. Often, these meetings take hours or an entire day to come to agreeable conclusions.

Let us continue with the feedback aspect raised by marketing. The production team has now become aware of the consequences of not responding immediately. They discuss amongst themselves and come to a consensual agreement to revert within 48 hours from the time a request is made. This is another understanding that gets recorded. A third flip-chart board captures the record of decisions between the two parties.

In the concluding session, the respective bosses go through the decisions put up on the third board. They take turns and address the whole group. The meeting ends with a feeling of satisfaction for all concerned.

This is termed a **two-party confrontation** meeting and is a very good intervention to get **Voluntary Active Support from people**.

Additional notes:

Other methods to improve inter-departmental harmony:

Bring teams together from the beginning: This way, teams will know how they should complete their workflows to help other departments complete theirs. Make sure everyone is on the same page: Team leaders need to acknowledge the places where their work overlaps with other teams. Then, there must be an understanding of their roles to make sure this overlap is seamless.

Encourage feedback:

- Build an environment in which they feel comfortable sharing their opinions.

- Ask the team(s) what's working and what's not.

- Regular feedback can help streamline intersections between departments.

Some fundamentals to promote inter-departmental harmony:

- Building relationships.

- Organising meetings periodically.

- Creating a common 'way forward'.

- Focusing on company vision and values as a binding force.

References

- *https://www.pandadoc.com/blog/10-tips-to-foster-efficient-inter-departmental-collaboration/*

- *https://smallbusiness.patriotsoftware.com/what-is-interdepartmental-communication-strategies/*

2. Sowing the Seeds of an SMT Way of Working

Self-management is a type of team structure that distributes decision-making power among team members rather than concentrating the power on one person like the manager. A self-managed work team is a small group of employees who take full responsibility for delivering a service or product through peer collaboration without a manager's guidance. A group of people work together towards a common goal, which is defined by stakeholders outside of the team. A manager or department head will define the overall direction and desired outcome and will provide the required tools, resources, and training if required. While this can pose some unique leadership challenges, it also offers leadership opportunities and skill development that may not be accessible to a traditional team.

There are several benefits of having self-managed teams:

- High motivation.

- Quick response and agility

- Low overhead maintenance.

- Enhanced innovation.

There are certain challenges faced by SMTs, and the reader can observe how they have been taken care of in a real-life example cited below by the author:

In the fan regulator section, twenty people were assembling close to 1000 regulators in a day. The mandate given to them was that there would be no supervisor who would oversee their work. They were asked to manage the raw material supply from stores, inform the maintenance department about any disruption in the process owing to mechanical or electrical problems, and, to top it all, take ownership of the quality of goods produced. They were given the freedom to set up the line by consensus amongst themselves.

There was a typical challenge to surmount: There was a sense of resistance from the operators themselves to the new way of working, where ownership was the key. (They were used to highlighting issues in supply or maintenance to the supervisor, who in turn would take necessary action. Till the time the problem is rectified, the operators would relax and gossip.)

Communication with the Union helped – they were informed that this is a harmless experiment that the organisation is conducting and that the results will not be binding on them. However, they could choose to continue the new way if they felt it benefited them and the organisation. The communication was carried out at two levels – one at the apex level of the union and the other at the local managing committee level. **In hindsight, we realised that the turning point of the experiment was this particular step**.

Another challenge bordered on the willingness of the shop floor management (foreman, superintendent), who in the beginning felt their jobs were at stake. This was mitigated by proper formal discussion to convince them and allay their fears.

The results we got in a matter of three weeks were phenomenal. a) There was a sense of heightened enthusiasm amongst the operators – they seemed to enjoy the newfound ownership. b) There was a 10% rise in productivity. They were now assembling 1100 pieces. c) Operators took extra pain to keep the area clean, and their housekeeping scores went up.

This experiment opened the door for a self-managed way of working.

The above experiment demonstrates and furthers the concept of getting voluntary active support from people – the mainstay of this book.

Some pertinent learnings from the process:

- Informal sounding with the team to explore possibilities before commencement.

- Providing guidance and guardrails.

- Defining team objectives and goals.

- Training the members on aspects of self-management.

- Demonstrating a pilot project of an SMT for smooth change management

- Providing ongoing support when needed without making the team dependent.

Self-managed teams are best suited to companies where the organisational culture actively supports autonomy, employee empowerment, and collective decision-making.

References

- *https://www.betterup.com/blog/self-managed-teams*

- *https://www.getclockwise.com/blog/self-managed-teams*

- *https://recruitee.com/articles/self-managed-teams*

3. A Culture that Promotes Teamwork

Teamwork is a sense of unity. A diverse group of people each brings a variety of skills, experiences, and viewpoints to any group or team. This variety of different skills and experiences come together in cooperation among those who are working together on a common task to achieve similar goals. Teamwork is possible when the work blends everyone's strengths to complement each other, while also bringing about a sense of camaraderie and shared vision among a group of people.

A successful culture of teamwork can be characterised as an environment marked by the shared belief that the organisation can move forward most effectively when collaboration and cooperation are at the heart of thinking, planning, and decision-making.

A good teamwork culture has five attributes:

Empowerment: Teams are encouraged to be self-reliant and empowered to make their own decisions.

High Expectations: Teams are given important assignments and projects.

Support: Teams with the talent and ability to produce results are supported by management with the time, budget, people, and other resources needed to do their jobs.

Encouragement: Teams are encouraged to work independently, and employees are encouraged to form their informal teams to solve problems.

Training: Teams have the proper training for their positions as well as cross-training opportunities.

Creating a teamwork culture is easier when it is promoted, sponsored, and supported from the top of the organisation.

In addition, there are three benefits.

- Employee Retention

- Higher Engagement

- Higher result orientation

Supporting factors for building a culture of teamwork.

- A good performance management system that distinguishes clearly between good performers and not-so-good performers

- A measurement system with adequate performance measures to know the progress against goals and periodic review of the same.

- Decision-making by consensus as a rule.

When team reviews are conducted and if no person is ready with the presentation as decided, there must be no penalty or loss of face. What can be done is to ask the person to present the next time. If this happens for three consecutive meetings, he/she feels ashamed. In such cases, most likely, he/she starts performing as an alternative to facing ignominy.

Another example that fosters team alienation, happens when the boss fires someone in the presence of his seniors, juniors, or peers. It hurts the person's ego, and this can prevent the person from contributing towards organisational goals. (Refer to chapter 11 on Managing subordinates.)

Some additional imperatives for establishing a teamwork culture:

- Establish effective team communication because it is the foundation of productive collaboration.

- Organise team-building activities because they will help teammates learn how to work together.

- Celebrate the team's successes because it will inspire teammates to continue thriving.

The recent pandemic has proved beyond doubt, that teamwork, is equally crucial in both situations - work from home or work from office. The above points can help in this regard.

References

- *https://www.michiganstateuniversityonline.com/resources/leadership/how-to-build-a-culture-of-teamwork/*

- *https://www.simpplr.com/blog/2021/how-to-create-a-culture-of-teamwork-in-the-workplace/*

- *https://www.smartrecruitonline.com/how-to-promote-teamwork-culture-in-the-workplace/*

Epilogue

In a manager's role, success or otherwise, depends to a large extent on the support from people working alongside. This book is an attempt to help professionals in this crucial imperative.

While the book details 9 + 7 = 16 ways of getting voluntary active support, the principles embedded therein are applicable to the workplace, social and home domains as well. One can say that this work is an attempt to understand and solicit supportive behaviour from colleagues, friends, family, and almost anyone we meet.

In an era where ChatGPT or other AI tools are used for book writing, the author has refrained from the same and written straight from the heart and the gut. Organic content in the form of his experiences and interactions in industrial and corporate life, spanning almost four decades, has been lucidly explained in this book.

Another point to note, is that readers, could have had their own experiences in regard to Voluntary Active Support, and therefore many more ways of getting VAS would be possible. The author invites examples to validate the methods outlined in this book, and in addition, if there are other ways in which readers have experienced mobilising support of people they live and work with. The author would love to hear from them via email id - kiyer49@yahoo.com.

Happy Reading!!!

List of Figures

About the Author

Dr Krishnamurthy Iyer is an engineer turned behavioural scientist with a career of over 40+ years – in operations for 16 years & HR for 27 years, in esteemed organisations such as Crompton Greaves Ltd. and Mahindra & Mahindra Ltd.

He is a qualified Mechanical & Electrical Engineer. After 16 years in operations (Production, Industrial Engineering, Projects, Materials Management, etc.), his passion for people development made him embrace Personnel Management and Industrial Relations & later HR at Mahindra & Mahindra Ltd. Post contributing as GM – HR for four plants of the Auto sector and a brief stint in internal communications, he retired as the Sr. General Manager for Learning & Organisation Development from Mahindra & Mahindra Ltd.

He is a keen student of human behaviour and still teaches at reputed management colleges. Initially, he taught engineering subjects like Productivity Techniques and Production Management and later HR subjects like Organisational Behaviour, Strategic Human Resource Management, and Organisation Structure & Design for post-graduate classes. His entire academic career spans over three and a half decades.

He also holds a Diploma in Management Studies from the University of Mumbai and a Diploma in Training and Development from ISTD, Delhi. He was awarded a PhD in Human Resources and Change Management from Birla Institute of Technology and Science, Pilani – in 1998. His thesis was "Adaptation of Japanese Management Practices to Indian Organisations – Some Studies."

He has presented several papers at National and International Conferences and is also certified as a "Grow More Coach" – having completed 80 hours of the approved and ICF accredited Grow More Coach Model training programme.

Dr. Krishnamurthy Iyer currently runs his consultancy, Kartikay Associates, which supports medium and small scale industries as a Strategy Mentor, OD and HR facilitator, and a mid-life success coach.

He can be reached by e-mail – kiyer49@yahoo.com.

His website address is www.kartikayassociates.com.

. . . . .

www.ingramcontent.com/pod-product-compliance
Lightning Source LLC
Chambersburg PA
CBHW020609160726
47991CB00002BA/694